JOHN MACLEAN

A FIGHTER FOR FREEDOM

Printed in *Scotland* by
KIRKWOOD (PRINTERS) LIMITED
152 Clyde Street, Glasgow, C.1

JOHN GRAHAM

JOHN MACLEAN

JOHN MACLEAN

A FIGHTER FOR FREEDOM

by
TOM BELL

COMMUNIST PARTY, SCOTTISH COMMITTEE
1944

TO PHYL

PREFACE

By Harry McShane

Scotland has every reason to be proud of its contribution to the development of the Labour and Socialist movement of Great Britain. This contribution has taken a variety of forms, trade union and political organisation, and theoretical and practical propaganda. Its more spectacular contribution, however, has been in the personalities who have distinguished themselves in advancing the movement. Of these no list can be considered complete that omits the name of the school teacher socialist John Maclean.

To the younger generation of socialists John Maclean is perhaps little more than a name. But those of us who belong to the older generation and who knew the man, who were privileged to be associated with him, to observe him in the course of his work, will always cherish a high regard for him as one of Scotland's socialist pioneers. His devotion to the cause impressed everyone with whom he came into contact. That he possessed the great qualities of ability, courage, and honesty was admitted by his strongest opponents. Even the judges who sent him to prison testified to this. He was prepared to make any sacrifice in order that socialism be understood by the masses and finally triumph in this country.

The political life of John Maclean coincided with the formative period in the modern labour and socialist movement. In those days to be a labour man, not to speak of being a socialist, called for the qualities of courage and steadfastness that come from conviction. A lot of spade work had to be done to get the ideas of labour and socialism accepted. Intense propaganda and education had to be undertaken to convince workers of the need for a political party independent of liberals and tories. Rights of trade union organisation, recognition of the union, collective agreements and many of those things we take for granted to-day had to be fought for, as the records of history show.

This book gives the reader a glimpse of those days. It then takes us through the period of the first world war and the first socialist revolution. It recalls to us the great propagandist activities of John Maclean, especially his educational work in spreading the teachings of Karl Marx and Frederick Engels, and his decided views on the part he considered the co-operative movement ought to play in assisting the cause of the working class and the people generally.

But though the name of John Maclean will always be associated with working class education, I think that those of us who lived through the hectic years of the first world war will always regard his stand against the war and his stubborn fight against the government of the day as of even greater importance in the life of Maclean. The honour and good name of international socialism was at stake, and it is to the eternal glory of Maclean that the great leader Lenin singled him out for special praise and distinction for his defence of socialism.

Since this book is appearing in the midst of a new world war it is important, as Tom Bell points out, to take note of the very different character of the present war as compared with the war of 1914-1918. The first world war was the climax of a sordid struggle for markets and spheres of investments which had long been going on between rival groups of finance-capitalists. An obligation rested upon all honest socialists to oppose it. And John Maclean fulfilled his socialist duty, as Liebknecht and other socialists fulfilled theirs. Moreover, the end of that war was hastened by the growing revolt inside Germany against the war lords.

To-day the situation is a different one. We have seen the rise of fascism, which is another name for the dictatorship of the most reactionary elements of finance-capital. It began with the systematic destruction of all democratic institutions in its own countries—trade unions, labour and socialist parties, co-operative organisations, liberal and independent intellectual thought and culture. It organised, above all in Germany, the deliberate and wholesale corruption of the masses of the population (with the exception of a courageous minority). It inculcated a false and arrogant delusion of their own superiority and hatred of other peoples ; it held out the prospect of unlimited plunder from the enslavement of other countries.

The peoples of these countries, their independent life crushed out, were to be transformed into working slaves for the benefit of the so-called " master race," to whom all things were permitted and whom no consideration of international law of decency or humanity should be allowed to restrain.

Fascism became an article for foreign export. Its political, economic, commercial and diplomatic institutions abroad became centres of espionage and corruption. Its agents penetrated everywhere with a view to weakening the democratic countries in every way and preparing its Quislings. It began the present war as a coldly calculated and cynically prepared attempt, headed by the Nazi Hitlerites, to subjugate the rest of the world to the self-styled herren-volk. In spite of everything it was still possible to hope, in the early part of this war, that some serious resistance would be offered by the German people to the ruling clique of criminal gangsters. But month followed month, and the Nazis crowned the successive iniquities by the invasion of the Soviet countries, the Socialist fatherland of all the world's workers, without any organised struggle against them at home. It became clear that the main burden of the task of smashing the German military machine and the Nazi regime would continue to fall on the United Nations allied against fascism, and that whatever chance there might be of rousing the German people to a sense of their heavy responsibility lay in the most rapid and thorough military defeat of Germany.

John Maclean opposed the war of 1914-1918 because he was against the workers slaughtering each other for the benefit of the capitalists and landlords. He was by no means a pacifist and opposed to war in all circumstances. I make bold to say that this man who devoted his whole life to the fight for the common rights and liberties of the people ; in whom individual rights and the defence of democratic organisations, the independence and freedom of nationalities, found a constant champion, who was an ardent defender of the socialist republics of the U.S.S.R., would if he had been alive to-day, have put the same zeal and enthusiasm he showed in 1914-1918 into the cause of this just war, to end fascism everywhere.

John Maclean served the cause of socialism regardless of self. He gave his all and sacrificed his health and life in his efforts.

In this respect he set an example to us all. In this outline of Maclean's political work, Tom Bell, who was closely acquainted with the man and played an active part in many of the events of the period, and is therefore well fitted to write the story, has brought out lessons from the period covered in the hope that we may avoid many of the mistakes made by the active men of the time. I hope that this book will be widely read by those who played some part in the movement of these early days, as well as by those who have come into the fight for socialism in recent years.

NOTE.—Since this work was written the author, Tom Bell, has passed away.

Tom was one of the pioneers of the movement on Clydeside, working for many years, under difficult circumstances, in order to further the cause of Socialism. It is fitting that his last job was to complete this work on the great proletarian leader, John Maclean. He corrected the proofs and brought them to Glasgow. Within a week, he died in Glasgow Royal Infirmary. It is to be regretted that he did not live to see the book in print, but we must be grateful for the fact that he was able to complete it.

H. McS.

AUTHOR'S PREFACE

THIS little book makes no attempt to give a complete biography of John Maclean ; it deals only with his political life. Even in this respect I am conscious of its limitations, partly from inadequate documentation, and partly for reasons of space.

The political life of John Maclean reflects the period when imperialism had matured, giving rise to international conflicts and wars. It is at the same time a period of rapid growth and development of the labour and socialist movement. John Maclean is essentially a product of these conditions. Teacher, propagandist and fighter, he acquired an international reputation, and gained high praise and honour from the Russian working class—in particular from its great leader, Lenin—for the fearless stand he made for socialism during the first World War, 1914-18.

Though he did not join the Communist Party of Great Britain, he nevertheless belongs to the great family of Communism. As such and as a true son of the Scottish people his memory will be revered by the working class movement in Scotland. To contribute a little towards the preservation of this memory has been my sole object in writing this book.

I wish to thank the numerous friends who have rendered assistance by advice and suggestions in arranging my material ; in particular Harry McShane and William Joss for reading the manuscript and their helpful remarks and Jackie Thompson for the use of his collection of Maclean's notes for " Lectures on Economics."

I owe a special indebtedness to Hugh Hinshelwood, who kindly sent me personal letters, newspaper cuttings, articles and numerous biographical details gleaned from his long associations and comradeship with Maclean.

T. B.

December 1943.

CONTENTS

CONTENTS

JOHN MACLEAN

A FIGHTER FOR FREEDOM

CHAPTER 1

EARLY LIFE

DANIEL MACLEAN, the father of the subject of this study, was born in Mull in the year 1845. The island of Mull was the original home of the Clan Maclean. History tells of the oppression of the Macleans by the Argylls, the rackrenting and expulsion from the island by fire and sword. In 1848, when Daniel Maclean was three years old, the encroachments on the area of soil under cereal cultivation was aggravated by a potato blight. The life of the crofters of Mull was miserable beyond description. A Highland Relief Board Report (1849) speaks of the inhabitants wasting away with hunger. Many of those who emigrated died of cholera on the high seas. In one instance, of 400 emigrants on one of these coffin ships only 15 reached the other side of the Atlantic.

It is not surprising that Daniel Maclean, like most of the young men of Mull, should migrate to the industrial south in search of a livelihood. He obtained work as a potter and appears to have been resident in Nitshill when he met Ann McPhee, a weaver in one of the cotton mills there and, like her husband to be, of highland extraction. Ann was a native of Corpach, a little village opposite Fort William, where she was born in 1846. The marriage took place in Nitshill in 1867. Like most working class families the Macleans had to move about in search of work and wages. For a time Daniel Maclean worked in Bo'ness, Linlithgowshire. Later he brought his wife and young family to Pollokshaws, where he found work in Lockhart's Pottery. John was born at King Street, Pollokshaws, on 14th August, 1879. Though we have no precise details about the economic situation of Daniel Maclean and his little family that year we do know that there was a great deal of privation among the working people of Scotland generally. For, in October 1878, ten months before John was born, the City of Glasgow Bank had failed, throwing tens of thousands of people out of work. Able-bodied men in Glasgow and other industrial centres were breaking stones, teasing oakum, or digging ditches to gain a pittance from the Relief Funds. Thus the young Maclean was cradled and reared in an environment of privation and hardship.

When John Maclean was born Pollokshaws was an independent township of the county of Renfrew. Situated on the Pollok estates, the property of the Maxwells, an old feudal family, the surroundings were still semi-rural, when the Macleans went to live in the 'Shaws. Shady country lanes led to the pleasant fields and wooded thickets abutting on Thornliebank, Kennishead, Busby and Giffnock. It was a town of narrow winding streets where dwelt handloom weavers, bleaching and dye-workers, some colliers and engineers, and office workers, the latter mostly employed in Glasgow. In such a self-contained town without traffic or transport save some horse-drawn coach, life was slow, easy going and parochial. Here the young Maclean grew up, in the shadow of the great city to which he was to give the best years of his adult life and for whose good bourgeoisie he was to become the best hated man in Glasgow.

Daniel Maclean died in the year 1888, still a young man of 43 years. There is no doubt that the insufficiency of nourishment when he was a child, the hard life of his early years, and the lack of material comforts in rearing a small family left its mark on Daniel Maclean and brought him to an untimely grave. And it would be surprising indeed if memories of the persecution of the Macleans, the sentiments engendered by the crofters' bitter struggle to gain a livelihood, aggravated by the wage-slave life of the potter, had not been transmitted to the young John.

On the death of her husband Mrs. Maclean was faced with a problem that has often baffled less tenacious than she. A young family of four children had to be cared for. Here we find traces of that high spirit and dogged determination so marked in her son John. She did not hesitate to return to the mill and work as a weaver, her occupation before marriage. She took employment in the Auldfield Weaving factory of Pollokshaws. She brought up her family respectably, making her two sons school teachers. John Maclean in later years informed his companion, James D. Macdougall, " that it was the knowledge of the sacrifice made, and self-denial endured, by his mother and sisters to enable him to be educated, that made him resolve to use his education in the service of the workers." And to this resolution he stuck to the end.

As is the case with most working class families, there are no diaries, note books, letters or dossiers to guide us concerning the early life of John Maclean. From the scattered fragments written here and there we gather that his school life was varied by household demands on his time and the running of errands to gain a few coppers to help his mother. From the ordinary board school John passed to the Pollok Academy, Queen's Park Higher Grade School. During the long summer holidays he found work with the Thornliebank Print Works, thus helping to eke out the meagre family income. Studious and serious by disposition, his mind turned to the teaching profession. Encouraged and assisted by his mother and sisters he became a teacher at Polmadie School, in the south side of Glasgow. While a pupil teacher he continued his studies, attending classes at the Glasgow University morning and evening, and finally graduated with the degree of M.A. For this degree he took, among other subjects, that of Political Economy—a subject of which he was to make so much use in his later years.

Glasgow University has high traditions in the moral, social and material sciences. John Maclean acknowledged this, and in his lectures often recalled it was in Glasgow University that the great Adam Smith laid down, in 1753, those principles of his that were to be published in 1776, entitled "An Enquiry into the Nature and Causes of the Wealth of Nations." From Henry Graham, in his admirable essay on Adam Smith, we learn that Glasgow had in those days a Political Economy Club presided over by the Lord Provost, to further the trade of the town with its 20,000 people, and that a Select Society was started in 1754 to promote the improvement of land, linen manufacture, shipping and art, and soon numbered 300 members.

One hundred years later, when John Maclean was a student, the University text book on Political Economy was still saturated with the ideas of Adam Smith, only somewhat vulgarised by the crude notions of modern professors. For example, Professors Stanley Jevons and Alfred Marshall were doing their best to smother the scientific teachings of Karl

Marx with spurious doctrines of " Spots on the Sun " as the cause of economic crises, and " Final Utility " as the measure of value.

At the beginning of the twentieth century Glasgow University sought to keep up its radical bourgeois traditions in cultivating studies in the social sciences. In addition to the academic teachings of the University popular evening lectures were given during the winter months on social and economic topics, and intended without doubt as a corrective to the growing current of socialist ideas at the time.

The critical mind of Maclean could not fail to be sharpened by the growing labour and socialist propaganda during the period in which he was studying for his degree, and in particular by the controversy over the justice or injustice of the Jameson Raid on the Transvaal and of the Boer War of 1899-1902. The young labour and socialist movement was pro-Boer. Agitational and propaganda meetings were held in all parts of the city of Glasgow and the uplands of Lanarkshire ; the centre of attraction at these meetings being an Ayrshire miner named Tom McKerrall, who had worked in the Rand as a miner and knew the conditions. Keir Hardie, with facts and figures which he published in the columns of the " Labour Leader," denounced the war with telling effect. So much so that a howling mob of jingoes smashed in the windows of the " Labour Leader " office in Glasgow.

Every thoughtful and enquiring young worker and student was bound to be influenced by the vigorous flood of socialist propaganda and anti-war agitation in those days ; certainly a spirited student like John Maclean.

Indeed, Maclean proved to be the precursor of a whole group of students who later emerged from Glasgow University to become socialist propagandists, teachers, writers and editors— James Maxton, M.P., Tom Johnston, M.P., now Secretary of State for Scotland, Rosslyn Mitchell, Harrison Maxwell, Hugh Guthrie, to name only a few. Many of these University graduates acknowledged the influence of John Maclean in winning them for socialism. But while Maclean took the rougher road of Marxism, and class struggle, the majority of the students followed in the wake of Keir Hardie and the Party of social reformism, the Independent Labour Party.

CHAPTER 2

ENTERS THE SOCIALIST MOVEMENT

IF the period of Maclean's birth was one of trade depression and destitution among the people, it had another and more encouraging side to it. It coincided with an awakening of the working class movement in Great Britain, particularly in Scotland. There were as yet few traces of socialist propaganda, but the demand for working men as parochial municipal and parliamentary representatives was becoming more and more vocal. It was stimulated by the agitation and unrest among the crofters for land reform which led to the formation of a Scottish Land and Labour League.

On the other hand in opposition to the Liberal Government, to its foreign policy and coercion in Ireland, numerous Radical clubs had grown up. It was in an attempt to bring about the unity of such clubs that on the initiative of H. M. Hyndman the Democratic Federation was founded in 1881. Two years later, in 1883, this Federation adopted a socialist programme, and in 1884 the name was changed to that of the Social Democratic Federation. The Scottish Land and Labour League at Edinburgh adhered as a body, and constituted itself the Scottish section of the S.D.F.

Branches of the new Socialist Party were opened up in several towns. Bruce Glasier, who was later to figure so prominently in the I.L.P., helped to form a branch of the S.D.F. in Glasgow in the early summer of 1884, and says in his book on " William Morris and the Socialist Movement," that the first official statement of scientific socialism in Scotland was made that year in Glasgow by H. M. Hyndman at a crowded meeting in the Albion Hall, College Street. But for the direct forerunner to the modern political labour movement we have to look, not to the S.D.F., but to a body known as the Scottish Land Restoration League.

At the general election in 1885 the Scottish Land Restoration League put several candidates in the field, James Morrison Davidson (Greenock), James Shaw Maxwell (Blackfriars), William Forsyth (Bridgeton), John Murdoch (Partick),

William Greaves (Tradeston), J. Martin (Camlachie). To these may be added the crofters' fight in Caithness, with as their candidate Dr. J. D. Clark, who had been connected with the first International Workingmen's Association, and in North-West Lanark that of R. B. Cunninghame Graham, the Scottish Laird, then a Radical. Dr. Clark was returned, but Graham was beaten by just over 1,000 votes in a straight fight with a Tory. The following year, in 1886, Graham won the seat, while Clark retained his seat at Caithness. These contests are generally regarded as pioneering battles for independent Labour representation.

In March 1888, an historic bye-election took place in Mid Lanark. This was the bye-election in which James Keir Hardie, who had become prominent as a miners' leader and had been preaching a " Christian Socialism " stood as an advocate of independent labour representation. It is indicative of the political trends within the working class movement of the period that the Labour Electoral Association endorsed Hardie's candidature with the reservation that this was to hold good only if the Liberals adopted him. Following the experience of this bye-election the Scottish Labour Party was founded in June 1888.

The Scottish Land Restoration League gave its allegiance as a body to the new party. R. B. Cunninghame Graham became its President, and Keir Hardie its organiser. Thereafter a persistent propaganda was carried on throughout Scotland for Labour representation, independent of liberals and tories. Keir Hardie and others carried the struggle over the border into England and waged a systematic campaign, inside and outside the British Trade Union Congress, against liberal-labourism and for support to the policy of independent labour representation.

Five years later, in 1893, at a Conference held at Bradford at which the Independent Labour Party was formed, Keir Hardie and his friends had expected to secure affiliations from trade unions, trades councils, and other labour organisations. In practice no national trade unions attended, and very few trades councils, the majority of delegates coming from political bodies. The idea of securing trade union affiliations and establishing a federal organisation had therefore to be abandoned, and the

I.L.P. became a Socialist Society based on individual member-ship. When at last the Trade Union Congress decided in 1899 to support independent labour representation a new federal body did arise—the Labour Representation Committee, which changed its name in 1906 to the Labour Party. There was henceforth no question of Trade Unions affiliating to the I.L.P. The I.L.P. remained a propagandist body, and as such was for several years the decisive driving force in the Labour Party.

The period is one of intense propaganda for labour repre-sentation and the ideals of socialism. A veritable crusade was led throughout Scotland in those years with all the fervour and fanaticism of a new holy religion. In Glasgow and other towns street corner meetings, hitherto unknown and regarded with suspicion for a long time by the more reserved and cautious workers, became more and more numerous. The villages in the countryside were visited by a corps of young men and women missionaries of the new faith, and colporteurs of its literature.

Around such personalities as Keir Hardie and Robert Smillie, coal miners, Cunninghame Graham, aristocrat, Shaw-Maxwell, journalist, George Mitchill, printer, Peter G. Stewart, brushmaker, Sandy Haddow, steel smelter and George Carson, Secretary of the Glasgow Trades Council, to name a few of the outstanding personalities, were gathering younger men, fluent propagandists and active trade union functionaries, who were in later years to come in on the tide of socialist propaganda and to gain distinction as " the Clyde Brigade."

The S.D.F. too had its galaxy of talent in William Nairne, the stone-breaker, James Connolly, municipal employee and Ireland's first socialist martyr, Robert H. Hutchison, shoe-maker, George Yates, engineer, J. Carstairs Mathieson, Falkirk school teacher, John Leslie, Edinburgh insurance agent, with a younger school growing up as earnest students and pro-pagandists of Marxism.

In addition to these there existed the Clarion Scouts, with its " Flying Squad " of young cyclists and ramblers who combined their week-end outings in the country with the distribution of all kinds of labour and socialist literature and the holding of public meetings.

The mining villages in Lanarkshire, Ayrshire, Fifeshire and the Lothians became living receptacles of the new gospel and

its literature. The " Labour Leader," " Clarion," " Justice,"
" The Socialist," gave voice to the varying ideas and views of
the different groups. The sale of pamphlets and books,
socialist, labour, rationalist, and scientific was enormous.
The adherents of the respective groups read, studied, and
discussed things with a seriousness that caused some heart-
burnings to the custodians in those days of the bourgeois order.
Victimisation and black-listing became all too frequent ; but
only spread the movement to new and hitherto untouched
places. It was a period of confidence, of high optimism and
enthusiastic conviction on the part of the militants in the
certainty of victory, and of a new socialist society.

By the time Maclean was in his late teens and becoming
interested in the working-class movement there were three
currents facing him. As we have seen there was the Labour
Representation movement which still retained elements of
liberalism in its policy and leadership. There was the Independent Labour Party which was opposed to all ideas of the
class struggle and Marxism. And finally, there was the Social
Democratic Federation, proclaiming as its faith revolutionary
socialism and giving its adherence to Marxism, albeit academ-
ically, dogmatically.

Maclean chose the S.D.F., but, as in the case of many of his
contemporaries, it was not Marxism that brought him to
socialism. In the course of a lecture he delivered in the
Pavilion Theatre, Glasgow, on 23rd March, 1913, he declared,
" I was not brought to socialism by Marx. I am a convert of
Robert Blatchford—all honour to Robert Blatchford for it.
He has given us the finest elementary introduction to socialism
that I know of. ' Merrie England ' is the primary school of
socialism, but ' Das Kapital ' is the University. A study of the
Marxian theory is necessary to anyone who wishes to take an
active part in Socialism."

When Maclean actually adhered to the Social Democratic
Federation is not quite clear. On his first arrest and trial in
1915 he declares, " I have been enlisted for 15 years in the
socialist army." From this statement it might be concluded
he was a member of the S.D.F. in 1900. But this is highly
improbable. The present writer was a member of the S.D.F. in
1902 and took an active part in the general work of that body.

I was familiar with the active social democrats in Glasgow. But I have no recollection then of the name of Maclean.

Nor can we accept the statement by his friend James D. Macdougall (printed in an election pamphlet during the Gorbals Election in 1918, giving some biographical details of Maclean's life) that John joined the S.D.F. in 1905. As we shall see presently, Maclean was already an active propagandist in 1905. The most circumstantial evidence on the point of time is the emphatic assurance given to us by Bob Inglis (who was then the active literature agent for the S.D.F. branch in the Gorbals and still alive) that John Maclean joined the S.D.F. two or three months before the split that led to the formation of the S.L.P. As the split took place in 1903 following the Annual Conference held during the Easter holidays, this places Maclean as joining the S.D.F. at the beginning of 1903 or the end of 1902.

There is a circumstantial note in a letter from Maclean written in 1918 in support of his friend and comrade Hugh Hinshelwood, who was then the socialist candidate for Portsmouth, which says : " Hugh Hinshelwood taught me how to fight when I was his lieutenant in our unemployed marches through the streets of Glasgow during the 'Xmas week of 1905." From this it is clear John was already active in 1905.

Symptomatic of the outlook of the social democrats in this period was the emphasis laid upon education in the teachings of Karl Marx. Only a socialist revolution could put an end to wage-slavery and the whole capitalist system. But how to bring about such a revolution ? The socialists answered that with an ignorant working class steeped in the belief of the indestructibility of private property in the means of production a revolution was impossible. Education was needed, and particularly education in the teachings of Karl Marx. The trade unions were steeped in their craft interests and only interested in wages and better conditions of wage-labour. On the other hand the labour leaders politically were for the most part liberals, and engaged in the old parliamentary game of tweedle-dee, tweedle-dum. Let the working-class come to grasp the teachings of Marx and the relations of wage-labour and capital would become clear. They would no longer be content with half-pennies up and pennies down ; they would no longer vote for liberal, tory, or liberal-labour trade union leaders, but vote the pure socialist ticket and make the socialist revolution. Thus the social revolution was to be a revolution of ideas.

The most talented of the S.D.F. leaders in Glasgow after the split was the stone-mason, John F. Armour. Armour was not only a staunch trade unionist (in later years he was to become an official of the Stone-masons' Society), but he was studious by temperament and a devotee of Marxian economics. He had been a lecturer in the study circles before the split, and now, with the new faithful followers of Hyndman and Quelch that remained, a branch was kept going in the South Side area. As part of the branch activities, Armour kept to the S.D.F. tradition of conducting a study class in Marxian economics every Sunday morning during the winter months.

There is no doubt this tradition of study classes found a ready response from the teacher Maclean—a form of activity congenial to his temperament and which was to become associated with his name in after years. He was a welcome addition to the extremely limited list of tutors in Glasgow. But it is not long before he is organising and teaching classes in Gourock, Falkirk, and in his home town, Pollokshaws, which he did in 1907-1908, in conjunction with James Burnett, a railway signalman.

Another of the first forms of activity in which Maclean was engaged was in the " Press Committee " which served the Glasgow branches of the S.D.F. The daily and weekly newspapers and magazines were systematically scrutinised and topical matters noted. Letters to the daily and weekly press on such matters were prepared and sent, treating them from the socialist angle. Manifestoes and literature for municipal elections were written ; " Scottish Notes " appeared in " Justice " every week for six years. As we shall see later this attention to the press was never neglected by Maclean.

The winter months ended, the study classes closed and the summer propaganda began. Outdoor meetings were held by the S.D.F. in St. Enoch Square on Sunday evenings. As speakers, besides Armour there were George Neil, a baker, George Durward, a tailor, James Johnstone, a docker, to these were now added John Maclean, the teacher. Maclean, however-did not confine himself to St. Enoch Square, but soon went farther afield—Hamilton, Motherwell, Edinburgh and Fifeshire. It is about this time that Maclean made his first journey across the border to Carlisle. This visit was no doubt undertaken at the invitation of one of the brothers Lothian, a socialist family in Carlisle of which three brothers were railway workers, and all active members of the S.D.F.

It is thus as teacher, writer and orator that Maclean enters the socialist movement bringing three valuable qualities, all of which were much needed in those early days.

CHAPTER 3

SOCIALIST PROPAGANDIST

MACLEAN had been drawn to the S.D.F. partly by his own intellectual conviction and temperament, and partly under the influence of the emphasis which the S.D.F. placed on Marxian teaching and education. There was a big difference between Maclean and the other teachers. The social revolution for Maclean was much more than a battle of ideas. It was a war of the classes, physical and serious, in which no quarter was to be given on either side. Accordingly, he did not confine himself to lectures in the class-room. Studies in Marxist theory had taught Maclean that the working class—the creator of surplus values in the labour process—is the victim of exploitation and robbery in the mines, factories, workshops, etc. But it also taught him that this robbery is not confined to wages and prices, *i.e.* to the purely economic relations between workers and employers. There was the social and political side to life.

As we shall see, Maclean early understood that for a good social life, education, housing conditions, lighting, transport, health, sanitation, open spaces, public halls, libraries were vital and essential. In short, attention to local municipal affairs was an important part in the activity of every socialist seriously bent upon improving the conditions of the working class.

With the zeal characteristic of the man he formed a branch of the S.D.F. in Pollokshaws. In conjunction with his friend James D. Macdougall a campaign of socialist agitation was started in the town ; public meetings, letters to the local press, the distribution of literature, etc., were organised. It was something of an innovation in this sleepy little town, and unexpected for the respectable and comfortable middle-class. The conservatives met the attack by a flood of leaflets of a scandalous nature against socialism and the socialists in Pollokshaws.

Maclean was not the man to take these attacks lying down. It was in this period he had his first conflict with the School Board authorities. During one of the Municipal Elections Maclean had asked for leave off on the day of the Poll to attend the polling booth, and watch over the interests of the Labour candidate. Permission was refused, so Maclean took French leave and stayed away. He was suspended for insubordination pending a decision of the School Board.

John refused to take the " sack " and went to his class work as usual. The School Board, loth to take drastic decision, decided that an apology to the Head Master would meet the case. In the meantime one of the anti-socialist members of the Board wrote an article on the incident in the local press, making an attack on socialism and alleging its demoralising influence on the schools. The consequence was that Maclean refused to make any apology to the Head Master until this member of the Board had made an apology to him.

John had a good record as a teacher and was on the best of terms with the children and their parents. He held a leading place in the reports of the Inspectors. With his amazing energy he carried on a big campaign against all the members of the School Board who had voted for his dismissal. The affair died out—a tribute to the shock tactics to which Maclean attached the highset importance in all his struggles.

The demand for the municipal control of public utilities was at the time part of the political stock of every good radical and Labour supporter. Such important utilities as gas, water, tramcars, maintenance of roads and bridges, and sanitation were still in the hands of private companies. As these things more and more came under control of the Town Corporation, so too the cry for municipal houses became a popular one in face of the insanitary houses and backlands which were a scandal and danger to the health of the citizens in the towns of Scotland.

No provision was being made by the Town Council of Pollokshaws for the increasing population and the demand for houses. The older houses occupied by the workers had degenerated into veritable slums. The landlords continued to draw increasing rents, but stubbornly refused to carry out any repairs. With the growth of unemployment that was openly to flare up soon, the housing question and rents became a burning topic in Pollokshaws.

A Housing Council was formed. This Council comprised delegates from Trade Union branches, the Co-operative Society, the Liberal Association, the United Irish League, the Social Democratic Party, and the Third Ward Committee. It advocated the building by the Town Council of suitable dwelling houses for the working class, and condemned the insanitary properties in the town.

The question of securing land for building became a special topic. Pollokshaws like other townships in Scotland, once owned large common lands. The story of how these common lands were filched from the people has been told by Tom Johnston in " Our Noble Families " and in his " History of the Working Classes in Scotland." We must refer the reader to these works for further details.

Pollokshaws still owned certain lands, the remains of the stolen common lands, on which houses could be built. But all suggestions in this direction were frustrated by the house-owners and their cronies who dominated the Town Council. Influential deputations in which Maclean took an active part, waited on the Lord Provost and the Town Council. They pressed for the direct building of houses by the Council on the town's own land, instead of giving the land to private persons, and the exercise of its powers to compel reluctant slum-owners to repair their properties. At the Municipal Elections in 1906 a labour candidate was put forward in the Third Ward. In a report to " Justice," organ of the S.D.F., Maclean says, " We did very well at the election in the First Ward considering that our comrade's election address was just issued six days before the election, and we had therefore time to hold only four meetings and no canvass. The P.S.A. (Pleasant Sunday Afternoon) and the Temperance Party are strong here just now, but whisky and beer won. The younger generation and many workers who had lost their votes through removals or failure to pay the rates in time are solidly in favour of Socialism. Some hooligans were bribed to upset us, but I got the crowd to go for them at the meeting we held after the declaration of the poll. We managed, by an open letter, to put out ex-Bailie Baird in the Second Ward because of his opposition to our housing policy. We have doubled our membership, and soon will touch 100. Not bad for a small town."

Maclean's interest in municipal affairs was not confined to Pollokshaws. All the towns in Scotland suffered from the parsimony in public expenditure on the social welfare of the people, in particular from the evils of congestion in housing accommodation. Disease was rampant and there were few Municipal Health Departments. Some towns had no Health Officers whatever. Local friends related facts and figures to Maclean, including examples of graft and corruption in local and municipal administration which he never failed to use in his public meetings.

We have already referred to the struggle of Maclean's mother, who had for reasons of economy to live in crowded conditions. We would add here that John's elder brother, Daniel, had died in South Africa, where he had gone for reasons of health. Out of his own experiences and that of his family, therefore, John Maclean felt all the urgency of the housing problem, and he gave it a large place in his municipal activities.

We find him in this period actively collaborating in the exposure, by leaflet distribution and public meetings, of the health conditions in Greenock, where the percentage of tuberculosis was relatively higher than in any other town in Scotland. A pamphlet was brought out called " The Greenock Jungle." This was an exposure of the conditions in the local slaughter house and the absence of any effective hygienic control. The upshot was an enquiry by the Local Government Board, which, however, aggravated the public feeling by conducting the investigations in private. An Inspector was subsequently appointed for the town's slaughter house, an office to-day regarded as indispensable. Out of all this activity a Greenock Housing Council was formed, largely on the initiative of Maclean in conjunction with a Mr. Allan, the United Presbyterian minister, a man who had been attacking the Town Council for its indifference to the housing conditions.

From the examples we have given it will be seen that John Maclean attached the greatest importance to such elementary socialist duties as parochial and municipal life, and within the limits of his own times and understanding showed that he at least did not look upon Marxism as a mere dogma.

CHAPTER 4

THE UNEMPLOYED

We have quoted Maclean's reference to " our unemployed marches through the streets of Glasgow during the 'Xmas week of 1905." Unemployment was rife that year in Glasgow, and steps were taken on the initiative of Hugh Hinshelwood and George Anderson, both social democrats and members of the Amalgamated Society of Engineers, to organise the unemployed. Demonstrations took place through the streets, and deputations went to the Town Council to urge measures of relief. The deputation was introduced by Councillor Joseph Burgess, the founder of the " Workmen's Times," who had settled in Glasgow, and the baker George Neil, of the S.D.F., who presented the case for those out of work. Typical of the anti-war feeling in those days were the remarks of Hugh Hinshelwood in moving thanks to the Council on behalf of the deputation. While in the waiting room he had noticed a large recruiting poster on the wall. He could not resist the temptation to make the contrast between the funds spent on the army and the parsimony shown to the unemployed. This was the first deputation of unemployed workers to the Glasgow Town Council in modern times.

In the absence of any municipal or Government assistance to the unemployed Maclean and his friends did everything they could to call public attention to the plight of those without work. The following incident is typical. A parade mustering about 200 unemployed marched to an afternoon service in St. George's Church, Buchanan Street, to the consternation of the congregation, which had had no inkling of the intentions of the unemployed. The following Sunday a special collection was taken up in the Church and a sum of Eight Pounds Fifteen Shillings was raised. This sum, with the collections taken during the week, were distributed amongst those who had consistently taken part in the marches.

Three years later, in 1908-09, the unemployed question again came to the front. Tens of thousands of unemployed thronged the cities of Glasgow and the industrial centres. Pollokshaws had its share of the unemployed.

There was no " dole " in those days. Those in the old trade unions received their benefits if they qualified, but for the large mass of the unemployed there was nothing except the workhouse. True, under the Unemployed Workman's act of 1905 there were Relief Committees, but it was like trying to draw blood from a stone to get help. Besides, the Government's grants were so niggardly.

The socialists headed the agitation and put forward schemes for municipal works, the construction of new houses, making of roads, etc., by the Town Council. Keir Hardie introduced a Bill in the House of Commons for the " Right to Work," but with no results. The feeling in the country expressed itself in the bye-election in Colne Valley, Yorkshire, where a young man named Victor Grayson created a sensation by being returned, in 1907 as a Socialist and Labour candidate. Grayson criticised the Labour Party in the House for their timidity and fears, and to the chargin of the labour members, made several scenes in the House, in the name of the unemployed. Suspended from the House he toured the country stirring up the feelings of the workers who had expected much from the liberal-labour successes during the general election of 1906.

Meetings, demonstrations and processions of the unemployed became the order of the day. The S.D.F. took an active part in the demonstrations in Glasgow. John Maclean, John F. Armour and other comrades were in the van of one such procession through the centre of the city, in 1907. As the head of this procession reached the Stock Exhcange Maclean suggested it would be a good thing to march inside. The word was passed down the ranks and the Stock Exchange was for once invaded by the workers whose lives and labour are the subject matter of those gambling dens. The crowd marched right round the floor of the building and out again into the streets. Alarmed at the agitation, the City Corporation took over a large peat bog at Palacerigg and set a number of the unemployed to work. This was Glasgow's first labour colony organised on the principle that the unemployed workers must never receive money for nothing, lest it undermine their morale, and what was of more importance, the fabric of the social system !

Maclean did not confine his activities to Glasgow and other towns outside his own. He was active in Pollokshaws urging the cause of the unemployed. In March 1909 " The Pollokshaws Review " states that " at the Council meeting the Provost continued his petty arrogance by impertinently interrupting Maclean, while acting as spokesman for the unemployed who are being treated shamefully." It was during these hectic days that James MacDougall, who was at that time Maclean's companion in arms, was dismissed from his employment for his socialist opinions and activity, just as Maclean was to be six years later. Young MacDougall was the son of the Lord Provost. He was employed in the local branch office of the Clydesdale Bank. One of the local slum owners, incensed at the activity of MacDougall and Maclean, sent a letter to the manager of the bank threatening withdrawal of his business unless MacDougall was removed. The manager wrote to the local agent, who interviewed MacDougall, and informed him of the letter he had received from the manager. Young MacDougall made no bones about his socialist convictions, gave an account of his activities, and refused to promise to alter the course of his conduct. Dismissal ensued. MacDougall's father, the Lord Provost, was a liberal and thoroughly disapproved of his son's opinions and activities. The affair was the subject of a good deal of talk in the town, much to the discomfort of the Lord Provost.

Again we see in Maclean the man of action. He was not contented with a public exposure. As he then wrote, " the instigators also may look forward to a hot life of it." And if by

c

this he meant public denunciation and exposure, they got it. To the trade unions throughout Scotland he proposed that they should transfer their funds from the Clydesdale Bank. The craft unions of those days were not very likely to respond to such an appeal for such a cause. What is important for us, however, is the light it throws upon the militant class views and temperament of Maclean in this early period.

Another illustration of the temperament and activity of Maclean may be judged from the following incident that took place about this time, in 1909. There was considerable ferment in Spain due to the opposition of the people to the scandalous Melilla campaign in the Riff. Riots took place in Barcelona and other towns. In the course of the repression by the government, Senor Francisco Ferrer, an anti-clerical and educationalist rebel was arrested and shot in Montjuich prison. The cold blooded judicial murder of Ferrer led to meetings of protest in this country, and to an incident in Glasgow in which John Maclean was involved.

The Workers' Educational Association had called a conference which took place in the Queen's Rooms, Sauchiehall Street, Glasgow, to consider the question of Adult Education. Between three and four hundred delegates attended from trade unions, co-operatives, etc. The late Principal McAllister of Glasgow University was in the chair. At the conclusion of the conference Maclean, who was present as a delegate, asked leave to move a resolution of protest, condemning the murder of Ferrer, but the chairman suggested it was outside the scope of the conference. When the delegates were dispersing Maclean managed to get about 100 to march to the offices of the Spanish Consulate. Being a Saturday afternoon the Consulate was closed, but this did not deter Maclean. From the steps leading to the offices he addressed a meeting denouncing the war in the Riff, and protesting against the murder of Ferrer.

The propagandist activities of Maclean in this period led him to visit several towns in Scotland. In the course of these activities he came into touch with Agnes Wood of Hawick. Agnes Wood was also active in the socialist movement. The community of ideas and interests in the labour movement subsequently ripened into something deeper, and they were married on 30th December, 1909.

To be married to an energetic active socialist propagandist calls for exceptional qualities on the part of the wife. In the case of John Maclean, who was in great demand all over the country as tutor-lecturer and public speaker, and who we may imagine spent a lot of midnight oil in the preparation of his lectures, personal life was bound to be subordinated to the calls of the movement. But Nan Maclean, herself a socialist by conviction, proved a worthy helpmate. Two children were born of the marriage—Joan on 19th May, 1911, and Nan on 17th April, 1913. No father could have been more devoted to his children than John Maclean. He worshipped those two girls, who in turn reciprocated their father's love.

In many respects Maclean was a puritan. He was serious minded and studious, a non-smoker and teetotaller. But even the strongest puritan is not without some flaw in his armour, and John Maclean was no exception. He could use strong language when necessary. He loved to go to a football match and cheer on the Queen's Park, the one remaining amateur club amongst all the professionals. It has been said that he has been known to forego a committee meeting to attend the match. But this was in the " peaceful days " before the first world war.

CHAPTER 5

LABOUR UNREST

THE ensuing years up to the war, 1914-18, were especially marked by considerable labour unrest. The prime reason for the unrest was the appalling poverty conditions due to low wages and the absence of any social security when unemployed, in sickness and old age. The disparity between wages and prices had been growing ever wider to the disadvantage of labour since 1896. Some idea of the conditions of the times may be gathered from the fact that 100,000 railwaymen were in receipt of less than one pound a week. The miners too were demanding a modest five shillings a day as a national minimum. Cotton and woollen workers were paid incredibly low wages.

Dockers were mere casuals and working conditions appalling. To aggravate all this the employers refused to countenance the growing trade unions or to negotiate with their leaders. In the case of the railwaymen the Conciliation Boards and schemes to deal with grievances simply didn't meet or dilly-dallied with questions submitted to them until the men's patience was exhausted. The companies flatly refused to recognise the union or negotiate with the union officials. Such was the case, too, with the dockers and transport workers. As for the miners, the coal owners refused stubbornly to recognise the Executive of the Miners' Federation of Great Britain as spokesmen for the miners. The high hopes entertained upon the advent of the Labour Party and its parliamentary victories in 1906 had cooled with the ineffectiveness of the labour leadership in the House of Commons. A strong current of opinion ran through the working class movement that there was too much hob-nobbing with the Liberals in Parliament. Moods of anti-parliamentarism crept into the militant section of the movement, and by 1910-11 open revolt in favour of direct industrial action took place. The next three years were marked by strikes and lock-outs of varying magnitudes.

Unrest permeated all sections of the labour and socialist movement. The Social Democratic Federation, which had changed its name to Social Democratic Party in 1908, was critical of the official leadership of the Labour Party. Inside the I.L.P. and the Clarion Scouts discontent was rife with the policy and behaviour of the parliamentary labour leaders. A more clear cut stand for socialism was demanded. But how was this to be realised ? By the formation of a new Party ? There could be little hope in that direction ; Keir Hardie, Philip Snowden, Ramsay MacDonald, J. Clynes, F. W. Jowett, J. H. Thomas, etc., were too busy literally cashing-in on their position as the new fledged labour parliamentarians. Full paged articles appeared regularly in the vilest of the capitalist newspapers, dailies and weeklies, denouncing direct action and singing the praises of parliament and the constitution. So, too, were the old guard of the Clarion, Blatchford, " Dangle," R. B. Suthers, etc. On the other hand, lesser known figures in the I.L.P., like Leonard Hall and Russell Smart, and Tom Groom of the Scouts, while coquetting with industrial unionism were at one with the social democrats, Quelch and Hyndman, in looking upon the Labour Party leaders as " whittlers away of principle to suit the conveniences of trimmers."

The critical tendency which had arisen was healthy, and had it been properly directed could have contributed in a large measure to push the Labour Party and the working class movement still further along the path of socialism. But instead of learning from the teachings and experience of Marx and Engels, as to the supreme task of patiently and persistently working together with those masses that made up the Labour Party ; of criticising their mistakes and helping them to learn from their own experience, the dissidents fell victims to their optimistic illusions and set about the formation of a new party, that was to be a real socialist party.

A socialist unity conference took place at Manchester on 30th September and 1st October, 1911. Delegates attended from branches of the I.L.P., Fabian Society, Clarion Scouts and the Social Democratic Party. Only the S.D.P. was repre- sented officially as a Party. The other delegates attended in their personal capacity or the representatives of small groups. Out of the Conference emerged the British Socialist Party, with a pure " socialist " programme. But in point of fact the main nucleus of the new party came from the old S.D.P. Very soon out of the wave of syndicalist and Industrial Unionist ideas disruption crept into the new party to weaken it further.

In the tumult and ferment of the times John Maclean kept to his faith, carrying on with his socialist propaganda meetings and economic study classes. One month after the Unity conference we find him reading a paper on " Co-operation and the Rise in Prices " to a Conference of Renfrewshire Co-operative Societies. This paper is historically important for the light it throws upon Maclean's social and political views and will be treated in full later on.

The critical international situation, the rivalry between German and British Imperialism in naval construction, and the danger of war had wide repercussions throughout the whole international labour and socialist movement. The Inter- national Congress at Copenhagen in 1910 had reaffirmed the resolution of Stuttgart. Nevertheless in England there was much confusion. At Copenhagen, while Keir Hardie was insisting that " The day war is declared all workers must cease work," Bruce Glasier, at the same Congress, was denying that capitalism was the cause of wars. He was declaring that " war existed long before capitalism. Bestiality is the cause of war between men, and this bestiality has existed since the beginnings of mankind." Blatchford and the " Clarion " were screeching for a bigger and better Navy.

The old S.D.F. had countered the Conscription movement, led by Lord Roberts following the Boer War, with the demand for a Citizen Army, *i.e.* the training of every citizen in the use of arms. In opposition to the caste of officers in the voluntary professional army, the S.D.F. demanded the right of the citizen soldiers to elect their own officers. The Citizen Army was also put forward later as the alternative to the Territorial Army initiated by Lord Haldane. Hyndman had, however, become a rabid anti-German. The whole movement was in fact confused between the extremes of pacifism, revolutionary syndicalism, the general strike, and chauvinist national defence.

Maclean followed the official line of the social democrats in demanding the Citizen Army. Already in the " Pollokshaws Review " for April 1909 there is an exhortation " To young men " which reads : " We advise you not to join the Territorials. . . . You are liable to be called out to shoot strikers. Remember Belfast ! Agitate with us for a Citizen Army, where all shall be trained whilst remaining Citizens."

But if he favoured a Citizen Army it was for other aims than those contemplated by H. M. Hyndman, as we may judge from his opening remarks to the Renfrewshire Co-operative Conference in 1911 where he struck a note of warning in declaring : " The times we live in are so stirring and full of change that it is not impossible to believe we are in the rapids of revolution."

The next few months seemed to vindicate the prognostications of Maclean. In January 1912 the cotton workers were locked out. Two months later in March, occurred the greatest strike hitherto in British history. One million miners declared a national strike to establish a minimum wage. The government, as Lenin wrote in June of that year, pretended to yield to the workers, acknowledged the *principle*, of the minimum wage, but as a matter of fact, took the side of capital and did not do anything to establish the minimum wage.

The B.S.P. carried on a big campaign of meetings in Lanarkshire in support of the miners. One can imagine the effect of such movements on John Maclean. With unbounded energy he was to be found rousing the workers and imparting to them that same spirit of optimistic enthusiasm he felt in himself. At meetings, in the course of his lectures and study classes, his special knowledge as a teacher of economics was brought into play, explaining and interpreting the spurious arguments of the mine owners and the government to large audiences of miners in Scotland, who stood firm against any compromise until the vacillation and weakness of the miners' leaders in face of the trickery of the government ended the strike.

The year 1912 was a busy one for Maclean. Apart from his activity in support of the miners he was the principal speaker at a May Day demonstration in Falkirk, before 2,000 people gathered in the Public Park. In the evening he addressed a crowded meeting in the Falkirk Town Hall. The West of Scotland District of the B.S.P. planned a big campaign of meetings during the summer months. In the first week in May he addressed three meetings. In the second week he was speaking in Stonehouse, at Paisley and Barrhead. Up to August he averaged three meetings a week and was the principal speaker that month at Stonehouse, where a huge demonstration took place in honour of the memory of Wilson, the Strathaven martyr for political reform.

His usual Economics Class was formed on 29th September, 1912. During the Municipal Election in November he was working like a trojan for the return of the B.S.P. Municipal candidate, Tom Canning, who got the then creditable vote of 540. For the remainder of that winter he was mainly busy on his lectures to his economic class. All these activities were tremendous for a man who had to earn his living as a school teacher.

At the close of the winter indoor lectures under the auspices of the Glasgow Clarion Scouts, he delivered a lecture on " Marx and his Message " (23rd February, 1913). After tracing the early life of Marx, and expounding his contributions to science and theory, Maclean ends on the following note :

" I want you to go home and read the works of Karl Marx. If you read one or two good books they will do more good to your head and your heart than a library of rubbish. What we want in this country to-day is an educated working class. The millennium, if it is to come, must come from an educated working class. To-day, you can be swayed by speeches and pamphlets. But the person who has studied Marx and has applied him to literature, to life in all its phases, can see things as they are. Do your reading and thinking for your-selves, and if you are honest you will come to see the greatness and beauty of Marx."

During the month of March 1913 the Pollokshaws B.S.P. was protesting vigorously against the behaviour of the Glasgow Town Council for not keeping its promises, given when Pollokshaws was annexed to Glasgow, to provide the 'Shaws with a public library.

In the month of July Maclean was one of a team of six speakers at a big demonstration on Glasgow Green, " to protest against the raising of the load line on merchant ships." The arrest of George Lansbury, John Scurr and Mrs. Cohen that summer was the occasion for protest meetings in which the arrest of Sir Edward Carson and Bonar Law for their inciting speeches was demanded.

In September Maclean was involved in a dispute in the Coalburn Co-operative Society where two employees, he held, had been unjustly dismissed. He exposed the local intrigues and attacked a local faction which was seeking to carry its vendetta against its rivals into the local pit and attempting to drive them out of the mine.

That same autumn a teachers' strike took place at Neilston, Renfrewshire, over the payments for Evening Continuation Classes. A strike committee was formed and pickets were posted at the schools to stop blacklegs. Behind the strike was " The Scottish Teachers' Socialist Society." From the fact that the secretary was a member of the B.S.P. and lived in Pollokshaws, in Auldhouse Avenue, next door to Maclean, we may reasonably infer that John had a hand in the organisation of the teachers in that dispute.

On 5th October his economic class begins for the winter session in the Good Templars Hall, Ingram Street, Glasgow.

The winter classes over, the usual public propaganda begins and Maclean is more active than ever. The B.S.P. ran a large number of candidates for the School Board Elections that summer with several successes, notably Aberdeen, Falkirk, Larbert and Newton Mearns. An interesting note in a report from Newton Mearns says : " Under stimulus of the Education Elections a branch of the B.S.P. is formed on 6th June, 1914. For years Maclean and MacDougall would come and talk for a couple of hours or thereabouts on the A.B.C. of socialism."

Under the auspices of the Kilmarnock Socialist Hundred, Maclean on 19th July delivered an address on economics, and the local friends note that " the police are taking an interest in our meetings that they did not do before."

That same month a strike of the tenters in a linen factory at Dunfermline breaks out. It being the holiday season for teachers Maclean was at Tarbert with his family enjoying the enchanting scenery of the mountains and lochs. With his customary enthusiasm and zeal he interrupts his stay at Tarbert to go to Dunfermline to help the strikers.

Regarding this strike here are Maclean's own words : " At the request of the Dunfermline Trades Council I went through from Glasgow on Sunday, 27th July, to help the locked out tenters in the linen industry.

" About four years ago I was also through, helping to get the woollen workers into the Textile Union, and shortly after that the tenters were paid in a manner different from the good old way. The people used to get an upstanding wage of 32/- to 33/- a week according to the employer. But this gave place to the present method of a wage of 27/- to 28/- with a bonus of 8d. to 10d. on every £1 earned by the women. Eventually the men found themselves getting less than their former standard wage."

Maclean goes on to explain how a deputation was sent to the management of the firm (Beveridge and Coy.). The management informed the deputation that the standard wage arrangement only held for three months. When the deputation informed him that other employers were paying the standard wage, the manager gave the deputation 14 days notice to quit the firm.

In the meantime the war was on, and a number of the men

left to go to work at Rosyth, the naval base. Maclean says :
" I have set myself at workgate meetings and evening demonstrations to get the blacklegs to desist, or to get the girls to
strike in sympathy with the men." But the strike faded out.
Back in Tarbert Maclean is so insensed at the defence made by
Sir Edward Grey *re* Britain's entry into the war that he chalks
up on the wall in letters large for all who may pass by to see,
" Grey is a liar." He returns to Glasgow to enter upon the
most exciting period of his life.

CHAPTER 6

OUTBREAK OF WAR

THE war found the official Labour and Socialist movement in
Glasgow, as elsewhere in this country, without a united policy.
The British Labour Party was at sixes and sevens. The
International resolutions to which it had subscribed were dead
letters. The confusion was worse confounded by the failure of
Ramsay Macdonald, as Chairman of the Parliamentary Labour
Party, to give a straight lead. In Glasgow the I.L.P., the most
influential section of the workers' movement, took the line of
neutrality and pacifism, following the teachings of Keir Hardie
and the propaganda of the I.L.P. for many years, for " Peace "
and " International Brotherhood " rather than war. To be an
absolute conscientious objector and to refuse to fight under any
circumstances became the hall-mark of a good socialist and
anti-imperialist.

The Citizen's Army idea of the Social Democrats had never
been more than a question of propaganda with them. And
when Hyndman and Blatchford became out and out jingoes,
the Citizen Army was identified with military conscription, to
which the socialists of Glasgow were definitely hostile in all its
forms. Moreover, the B.S.P. was never a force in Glasgow,
although the indefatigable John Maclean was its outstanding
representative.

The other socialist groups were equally confused in the first
months of the war on the questions of resistance to the war,

national defence and pacifism. Thus there was a general mood among the militant workers of anti-war feeling, but there was no unified direction or centre of resistance. Socialist meetings went on as usual at their accustomed sites in the city, amidst interruptions and an increasing number of free fights with " students " and groups of " Patriots."

As we shall see it took several months under the stimulus of a fight for the defence of meetings and the rights of free speech, coupled with the unrest arising from the growth of economic demands, before some measure of common action was attained. Even then the common action was largely industrial and economic in character. True, the unrest had political consequences for the government, but no single political party emerged as a leader, it being tacitly agreed to subordinate parties for the greater aim of industrial unity.

The first public anti-war demonstration took place in Glasgow Green, 9th August, 1914. It was held under the auspices of the Labour and Socialist organisations and the Peace Society.

The aims of the demonstration were :
(1) To demand an armistice.
(2) To protest against the Food prices.
(3) To call for Government Distribution of Food.

There were several platforms from which representatives of the different organisations, judiciously grouped, spoke. The I.L.P. and the Peace Society speakers were concentrating their attacks upon the diplomacy of Sir Edward Grey, the evils of war, and the virtues of peace.

There was one platform predominantly B.S.P., presided over by James D. MacDougall, the companion of Maclean, and including, among other speakers, the present writer.

It would not be out of place perhaps to quote here some of our remarks as reported then in the Glasgow " Forward." MacDougall said : " The working class did not want war. They had no quarrel with Germans or other workers. The war was a capitalistic war and could benefit the profiteers only. The people who stood to gain by war were the armament rings." Thomas Bell said : " That war was the outcome of capitalistic greed, the outcome of the hunt for trade. It was possible, and very likely, that Russia was instigating Servia to force Austria into declaring war. If so, that desire had been accomplished and to-day we were witnesses to the alliance of Britain with Russia, the land of tyranny. These wars were based on force, the force behind the gun in the possession of capitalism. It was up to the workers to get control of that gun, and make wars no longer possible."

A number of the leaders of the B.S.P. were following in the chauvinistic wake of H. M. Hyndman. An article appeared in " Justice " about this time by Belfort Bax exhorting everyone to hate the Prussian military and bureaucratic system. John Maclean took up Bax's arguments and from an article which he published in Glasgow " Forward " in October 1914 we get the first concise account of Maclean's views on the war. He writes : " Our first business is to hate British capitalism." Analysing the arguments as to who's to blame, he goes on :

" Even supposing Germany is to blame, the motive force is not the ambitions of the Kaiser, nor the brute philosophy of the Prussian militarists, but the profit of the plundering class in Germany. Colonial expansion was denied the Germans because the British, the Russians and the French had picked up most of the available parts of the world."

He goes on to refer to what he called the cant about Prussian militarism when Britain led the world in the Navy business, and says :

" Plunderers versus plunderers with the workers as pawns doing the murdering with right good will. The working class at home is beginning to starve and is being buoyed up with the assertion that this is to be the last war.

" Unless a social revolution bursts forth in Europe at the close of the present murder campaign . . . we may have another war.

" It is our business as socialists to develop a ' Class patriotism,' refusing to murder one another for a sordid world capitalism. The absurdity of the present situation is surely apparent when we see British socialists going out to murder German socialists with the object of crushing Kaiserism and Prussian militarism. The only real enemy to Kaiserism and Prussian militarism is German Social democracy.

" Let the propertied class go out, old and young alike, and defend their blessed property. When they have been disposed of we of the working class will have something to defend, and we shall do it."

It may not be out of place here to remind the reader that this was written twenty-eight years ago, and in conditions of a war of another kind to that which is raging to-day. The purely imperialist character of the war in 1914-18 is not gainsaid even to-day, whereas the world war of to-day is a just war against the dark forces of aggression, terror and murder by a fascist clique that would throw civilisation back for centuries and destroy all democratic institutions, in particular the labour, trade union, co-operative movement—the very things Maclean treasured.

These views of Maclean corresponded then with those of the Marxists and Leninist Bolsheviks who were to translate them into deeds and with such tremendous significance for the generation of our time. From what we know of John Maclean, his class outlook, his hatred of tyranny and despotism, his comradely esteem for the Russian people and the Soviet Union, we have no hesitation in declaring our belief that were he living to-day, there would be no greater fighter against fascism than he. But to our narrative.

In the meantime Maclean's study classes go on. In Govan a joint committee is set up between the B.S.P. and the I.L.P., and meetings are held on " Social Problems in War Time." Maclean is addressing meetings for the I.L.P. on " War : Its Causes and Cure."

On 24th October a large conference took place in the City Hall Saloon, and was presided over by Robert Smillie, the miners' leader. At this Conference four ten-minute papers were read on a series of resolutions demanding :

(1) Higher standards of relief.
(2) Larger representation of working class organisations on the Advisory Committee of the National Relief Fund.
(3) Expedition of Municipal and other contracts to foster employment.
(4) On feeding and clothing of school children.

The resolutions of the Conference demanded :

(1) Adequate maintenance.
(2) Compensation for invalids.

(3) Pensions for persons disabled.
(4) Pensions for widows and dependants.

The growing ferment in the working class movement and the need for every organisation to define its attitude officially and publicly to the war led to an aggregate meeting of the B.S.P. in Glasgow, which took place on 3rd January, 1915. At this meeting the following resolution was passed :

" That this meeting of Glasgow members of the B.S.P., recognising that this war has been brought about by the intrigues of the capitalist and landlord interests of all the countries involved ; and that the workers of the world will obtain no advantages out of the war, determines to do all it can to peacefully stop the war at the earliest moment."

This resolution may be said to summarise the views of John Maclean on the war.

The bourgeois class as a whole regarded the war as an opportunity to speculate in values and get rich quick. In the first months there were no legislative restrictions. Prices in food, coal, and house rent began to soar. Fortunes were being made in shipping while the owners lay in bed. There was the example cited by J. R. Clynes in his Memoirs of one vessel which had been rusting in dock for years. It was given a coat of paint and sold for £20,000, sold again for £50,000 within a week, and again for £90,000 a couple of months later. All this time it did not put to sea. The house factors too were active in raising rents. At a meeting in January 1915 of the Glasgow House-owners' Association the Chairman declared : " a rise of rents was long overdue because of the accumulating burdens, increased taxation, interests on bonds, increase in tradesmen's wages."

The Scottish T.U.C. instituted an enquiry into the rising cost of living. It issued a special statement drawing the attention to the lowering purchasing power of wages due to increased prices, which it computed at 19 per cent. since the war began.

A large meeting was convened in St. Mungo Hall, South Side, Glasgow, by the labour and co-operative movement on the " Cost of Living." A strongly worded resolution was passed, demanding, in view of the increase in prices of food caused by extortionate freights and private speculation, and high prices for coal, that the government take over the food, coal supplies and shipping services. The same meeting protested against the increase in rents and called upon the government to prevent owners, by Order in Council, from taking advantage of people at this time, and upon the Town Council to establish a Fair Rents Court.

This meeting was followed up by a Conference convened by the War Emergency Workers' National Committee on 20th February, 1915, in the Co-operative Hall, Clarence Street, Glasgow. At this conference strong criticism was directed against the leaders of the Labour Party, especially Arthur Henderson, who was denounced as a recruiting agent for labour's traditional enemies, Bonar Law and Asquith. The demand was made for Henderson to come off the Recruiting Council until the government had taken steps to put an end to the extortion and robbery that was going on—an echo of the views of Maclean and the socialists. The Conference passed a strongly worded resolution demanding a reduction in fuel and food prices and of house rents.

In the meantime increased wages were being demanded by dock labourers, coppersmiths, boilermakers, locomotive workers (Hyde Park and Atlas works), carters and seamen and the brassmoulders, and, of course, the engineers. The general atmosphere had become electric among all sections of the working class movement. Meetings, conferences, discussions were going on everywhere. Hundreds of workers gathered around the various meetings held all over the city by the different sections of the socialist movement. Amongst these were the large gatherings around the platform of John Maclean every Sunday night in the centre of the city.

The demand of the Clydeside Engineers for an increase in wages of 2d. per hour had been pending when the war broke out. Finally the Conference between the North-West Engineering Trades Employers' Association and the representation of the Clyde district of the Amalgamated Society of Engineers met in Glasgow on 19th January, 1915. After three days' discussions no agreement could be reached. The negotiations terminated and the question was referred to a Central Conference of the Engineering Employers' Federation and the

Executive Committee of the A.S.E. This appeal for a Central Conference was made in conformity with a temporary agreement under the " Provisions for avoiding Disputes." The Employers suggested 12th February as the earliest date of meeting. In the meantime, the employers met in conference the representatives of a number of smaller unions, who had also demanded 2d. per hour increase—toolmakers, steam enginemen, machinemen's association—and offered them an increase of a halfpenny per hour, which was declined.

A great mass meeting took place in St. Andrew's Halls on 26th January. At this meeting resentment was expressed at the refusal of the claim and the delay in the National Conference. It was decided to stop working all overtime. By the 28th January 14 or 15 shops stopped working overtime. The District Committee of the A.S.E., instructed the members to continue working as before pending the decision of the National Conference. Representatives of the Executive Council of the A.S.E. rushed up from London to Glasgow with the object of trying to influence the members to change their decision, but they met with no success in Glasgow, though some outlying branches did abide by the District Committee's ruling.

The wages appeal was heard at the North-Eastern Station Hotel in York on 12th February. The result of the negotiations was a "mutual" recommendation of an advance of ¾d. per hour in the Clyde District ; this recommendation to go to the Ballot Vote of the engineers. In the meantime a dispute between the workers and the management of Weir's, Cathcart, came to a head. This firm had brought over from its works in the United States a number of workers and were paying them 6/- a week more than the other men in the shop. The refusal of the firm to concede the demands of the men coincided with the decision of the York Conference, and on 16th February 2,000 engineers struck work. (It should be said here that the American workers came out with the others, refusing to be strike-breakers.) A meeting of Weir's men took place in the Couper Institute, Cathcart, and there it was unanimously decided to stay out until their demands were granted. The strike spread and within three days eight other establishments had stopped work. Eventually 10,000 men were out. To conduct the dispute a strike Committee was set up, representative of the different shops. This was named the Labour Withholding Committee, and became the precursor of the Clyde Workers' Committee. Alarmed at the dangerous situation which had developed, the Executive Council of the A.S.E. took action and sent its representatives to Glasgow. A mass meeting was called and took place in the Palace Theatre. At this meeting the Executive members tried by every means to persuade the men to return to work, but without success. The Government also took immediate action. It appointed Sir George Askwith (Board of Trade), Sir Francis Hopwood (Admiralty) and Sir George Gibbs (War Office) as a Commission of Enquiry. This Commission sent up Macnamara of the Admiralty to enquire and report. He met members of the District Council of the A.S.E. and returned to London. The result was the appointment by the Government of this Commission to the status of a "Court of Reference;" in other words a Government Court of Arbitration.

By 25th February the ballot vote was decisive. The overwhelming majority of the engineers—8 to 1—voted against accepting the "mutual" recommendation. The Executive Council of the A.S.E. made yet another attempt to end the strike. William Hutchinson, the future pseudo-left of the Executive, was sent to Glasgow. At a meeting held at Whiteinch on 1st March Hutchinson is reported in the local press to have said, referring to the attitude of the Government : "If the men did not resume work they would probably be compelled to submit their case to compulsory arbitration, and once that principle was admitted the workers' weapon of the strike would be gone. If the men resumed work immediately it might be possible to arrange terms with the employers without recourse to arbitration. In that way the men would have an opportunity of voting on any offered advance, but if the matter was referred to compulsory arbitration they would have to accept the award of the Court whether they liked it or not. . . . . He understood that Lord Kitchener and the War Office were behind it." (Footnote, "Evening Times," 2nd March, 1915.)

This play by Hutchinson upon the threat of compulsory arbitration was a mean card of the Executive Committee. They knew that if there was one thing more than another upon

D

which the whole labour movement was united upon it was resistance to compulsory arbitration. Such a measure had always been held to be the negation of the rights of independent trade unionism. Compulsory arbitration was regarded as a form of industrial conscription, and conscription in any shape or form was anathema to the Glasgow workers, who had been nurtured on the socialist doctrine of a free and independent working class movement. To raise the threat of compulsory arbitration was verily the last hope of an Executive that was bent on playing the role of strike-breaker.

A combination of factors eventually led to a resumption of work, by 4th March. Chief amongst these were : the resistance of the Executive Council and the District Committee ; the inability of the Clyde men to get unity with other districts in England, where by local agreements certain small increases of wages had already been granted ; the government's intimidations and threats of conscription in to the army, backed up with an offer to submit the claim to a Court of Arbitration as soon as work was resumed.

Realising the inability to hold out and rather than risk a debacle, the Strike Committee at a mass meeting of the strikers recommended a resumption of work. After the resumption of work there were attempts in some shops to carry out the recommendation of the mass meeting for a " stay-in " strike and " ca-canny," but there was no longer the will and determination to go through with such a policy. Nevertheless, a deep sense of class feeling had been generated which expressed itself markedly in several directions throughout the course of the war, in particular by the emergence of the Clyde Workers' Committee, which grew out of the Central Labour Withholding Committee.

But if anything was calculated to fray the temper of the workers and to fan their sullen resentment into open revolt it was the Munitions of War Act (July 1915). Many workers had already booked their rooms for the Glasgow Fair Holidays. Intimidated by the uncertainties of the new Acts holidays were in many cases cancelled. But this was only the first detrimental effect of the new Act. They soon experienced others.

Under the Act it became a penal offence to leave without the consent of the employer. It was a penal offence to refuse to undertake a new job however low the wage rate or piece rate. To refuse to work overtime whether extra time was paid or not was an offence. A worker could not leave, even after giving notice, to go from one Munitions shop to another, however low his wages might be. On the other hand the employer was not bound to give work or wages. Men were told to stand-by waiting for materials, losing hours and days, but employers refused to give leaving certificates without which no one could employ the worker. Before the Munitions Tribunal 60 to 70 cases were being heard every day of the week. The Chairman of the Tribunal could pronounce a sentence against which there was no appeal.

Such restrictions upon industrial labour rights and personal liberties were in flagrant contradiction to the traditional rights of the working class movement, and demanded sacrifices for a war which the militant trade unionists and socialists looked upon as a struggle between rival imperialist groups merely for territory and trade.

The unofficial movement which had died down somewhat after the Engineers' (February) Strike began to regather strength. It received a new impetus from the arrest of one of the militants in Parkhead Forge. This was the Marshall case. An engineer named Marshall had struck a non-union man in the jaw and laid him out. It was, to say the most of it, a case of assault. But the utmost use was made by the prosecution of the cry of " slacking " and " ca' canny " and Marshall was sentenced to three months' imprisonment. Funds were raised for the support of Marshall's family, and preparations were being made for a strike when he was liberated.

From this moment steps were taken to enlarge the Unofficial Committee, which had so far been confined to engineering and shipbuilding workers. Now railwaymen and miners were included. Very soon another case was to bring fresh confidence to the reviving mass movement. This was the Fairfield case.

One day in October 1915, one of the managers in Fairfield Works saw one or two shipwrights standing-by, waiting to get work. He ordered the dismissal of two men. They were given their clearance certificate, but the reasons for dismissal were clearly marked on them. This was the old hated " Document," which the Trade Unionists of a generation back had fought to

abolish. A strike occurred in support of the two men. Seventeen men were brought before the Munitions Tribunal and
fined £10 each or one month in prison. Fourteen of the men
paid the fine, but three of the seventeen refused to pay on
principle. They were socialists. They preferred to go to
prison for a month, as they rightly believed that the payment
of the fine implied recognition of the Acts, and admission that
they were criminals. There began immediately a great movement for their release.

The Govan Trades Council issued explanatory circulars and
forms of resolution of protest. Eventually a large delegate
meeting took place representing some 97,000 workers. From
this meeting an ultimatum was sent to the Government that
if the men were not released in three days there would be a
stoppage of work. The next day it was announced that the
men's fines were paid. But by whom? Certainly not by the
men or any of their friends. It was suspected then that either
the officials of the Trade Unions had paid them, or the government had ordered the release of the men or there had been
collusion of officials and government.

The cumulative effects of the rising cost of living contrasted
with the profiteering going on, the restrictions and punitive
measures imposed upon the workers by the Munitions Acts and
the Defence of the Realm Act, coupled with the handing away
of the powers of the Trade Union Executives under the
Treasury Agreement, was by this time crystallising into deep
widespread unrest and into direct action by the workers. This
brief sketch will provide the reader with the background for
what we are to witness in connection with the activity of John
Maclean.

CHAPTER 7

FIRST ARREST OF MACLEAN

By the end of 1914 an opposition within the B.S.P. to the war and to recruiting for the forces began to take definite shape.

An Executive statement issued by the B.S.P. on 15th September, 1914, declared : " The British Socialist Party, whilst working consistently in the interests of peace, has always maintained the right of nations to defend their national existence by force of arms. Recognising that the national freedom and independence of this country are threatened by Prussian militarism, the Party naturally desires to see the prosecution of the war to a speedy and successful issue. . . ."

After demanding adequate provision for the wives and dependants of recruits ; national control and distribution of food ; abolition of militarism, armaments and secret diplomacy, the manifesto concludes :

" The British Socialist Party advises its representatives who are invited to take part in the general recruiting campaign to accept such invitations provided they are permitted to speak from the common platform in support of the national programme and policy set forth above."

There had been opposing views inside the Party from the very beginning on the character of the war. With the publication of this Recruiting Manifesto resolutions of protest were sent to the Central Office from a number of branches.

Maclean's views were crystal clear as we have seen from his reply to Belfort Bax in the " Forward." In Glasgow he was already carrying on a struggle against the views of Hyndman which were supported by Fred Cater, an old social Democrat and shoemaker from Northampton, a man well versed in the academic teachings of Marx.

The anti-war tendencies of the B.S.P. received a decided stimulus from the chauvinistic zeal of H. M. Hyndman. The I.L.P. had been distributing leaflets and pamphlets against the war. These publications had received some notice by " L'-

Homme Enchâiné." a paper edited by Clemenceau, the French
statesman who played a prominent role during the war, and by
" L'Humanité," organ of the Socialist Party of France. On
1st March, 1915, Hyndman sent a letter of protest to Clemenceau, and followed it up by another which was printed by
Clemenceau on 17th March, 1915. Here is the text :

6th March, 1915.

Dear Sir,

You will find with this note a brochure of the series of pro-
German pamphlets which is published now at great expense by
the Independent Labour Party—not the Parliamentary
Labour Party—Ramsay MacDonald, Keir Hardie, W. C.
Anderson, Bruce Glasier, etc.

This is a serious work ! This pamphlet is filled with revolting
lies. I am devoting all my efforts to make this understood.

Unfortunately, the writers of " L'Humanité " support the
Party, Independent of labour, *against the real workers of the
Social Democratic Federation* in attempting to show that the
Party, Independent of labour, is really the good side in this
terrible war. There is no certainty and we are curious to know
where it is getting the money for all its publications in favour
of the Germans against the Allies.

Very sincerely yours,

H. M. HYNDMAN.

This letter, says Clemenceau in a footnote, " is accompanied
with a brochure published by the Independent Labour Party
upon " The Origin of the War," in which the truth is highly
distorted by the grossest German lies. If the fact is contested
we shall be ready to demonstrate it."

At a meeting of the National Organisation Committee of the
B.S.P. a resolution of protest against the action of Hyndman
was carried. John Maclean associated himself with this
protest. While denouncing Hyndman Maclean made it clear
that he was far from satisfied with Hardie and MacDonald,
but, he said, " I would rather have my tongue cut out than
suggest the utterly base thought attributed to Hyndman—
that MacDonald, Hardie and company were acting as paid
agents of German Imperialist capitalism."

Maclean's views on the war were now in flagrant opposition

to the official policy of his party, the B.S.P., as reflected in the party organ, " Justice." Another kind of paper was needed and in September 1915 it appeared in the shape of the " Vanguard," a monthly paper described as being " Issued by the Glasgow District Council of the B.S.P." Articles, letters, etc., to be sent to John Maclean, 42 Auldhouse Road, Pollokshaws.

In a letter, 9th October, 1915, to his old friend and comrade Hugh Hinshelwood, of Greenock, Maclean says :

" We did very well with ' The Vanguard ' last month. We sold about 3,000 and cleared a slight profit. Our Economic Class enrolled 227 members the first day and in spite of the Hardie Memorial at St. Andrew's Halls we had a full house at the Panopticon. If we can keep it up the ' V ' should sell all right.

" I enclose a copy of No. 2.

" I see in to-day's " Herald " the result of the ballot. I regret your relatively small vote. For the sake of the rank and file movement now growing in the city I should suggest you might lend your influence to return Tom Clark.

" We have arranged that he and Messer speak at the Panopticon soon. We hold that the return of Clark will help to show the Clyde feeling against the Munitions Act. We have already said that the defeat of Gorman would indicate that. Your personal feelings apart, I would like you to view it in that light and act accordingly. We are building up a vigilance organisation on the basis of the Glasgow District A.S.E. shop stewards. I've tried to get the miners in S. Lanark to take similar steps and link up.

" I think the time has come when the shop, railway and mine workers in the Clyde basin ought to be directly linked together.

" I fancy you would do yourself the best favour—in the end—by trying to get the Greenock district built up on similar lines and linked up with Glasgow. Messer of Weir's, Cathcart, is the General Secretary, but I haven't his address beside me.

" Trust the ' Vanguard ' will be pushed in Greenock.

Yours frat.,

J. MACLEAN."

The appearance of the " Vanguard " carried into Scotland
the first open breach within the B.S.P. against the leadership of
Hyndman and his group. It ceased publication after five
issues, in January 1916, when it was seized together with the
" Forward " and the printers raided. The subsequent
adoption by the B.S.P. of the " Call " in February 1916, and
the break with Hyndman in June of the same year, made the
publication of " The Vanguard " unnecessary.*

In the first editorial, written by Maclean entitled " Our
Prospects and Policy," the reason for issuing " The Vanguard "
and of course, explaining Maclean's views on the war, are
stated as follows :

" Until the eve of this European murder contest the B.S.P.
in Scotland issued a free monthly tract called " The Vanguard.' For excellent reasons that venture ceased with the
outbreak of the supreme bestiality. Unfortunately for the
cause of socialism " Justice " from momentary paralysis proceeded to active support of the British capitalist class in the
attack on Germany, very largely under the influence of H. M.
Hyndman. To substantiate its support it threw overboard the
' materialist conception of history,' the compass of thorough
socialists in directing their activities in the accomplishment of
the overthrow of world capitalism."

After expressing the hope that " The Vanguard " might
become a thorough-going socialist daily the leader proceeds :
" Our object is the education of the workers into a clear
knowledge of the slave position they hold over all the globe
to-day . . . . With the aid of every socialist not afraid to do
and die for his principles, we intend to hammer into the head
of the dullest and most indifferent worker his brutally abject
position. . . . Nothing but world socialism will do. This
monstrous war shows that the day of social pottering or reform
is past. . . . The ' social reformer ' must be absolutely crushed,
for intolerance to him is but justice to humanity. . . . Capitalism, that is the right to rob the creators of wealth, must be

* In May 1920 the " Vanguard " reappeared as the personal organ
of John Maclean, he then being no longer in harmony with the B.S.P.
which was moving towards unity with other groups to form the
Communist Party of Great Britain.

killed, and it can be done in twelve solid months, starting any time, if but the workers are ready."

The workers have massed themselves practically into three distinct movements, says Maclean, the Trade Union, the Co-operative and the Socialist movement.

" Trade Unionism," he says, " up to the present, has been a defensive movement. The workers' position has been slightly bettered, whilst the capitalists' has been immensely improved. While from this point of view it has failed, trade unionism has kept the workers together and enabled socialists to vastly swell its numbers.

" Our policy will be the advocacy of Unions by industry, and unions of these Unions on a world basis with a world cord system—keeping pace with the trustification of the money power, and the using of these unions towards a complete control of the organisation and running of the workshops, mines, and land of the world. We are not for the absolute control of each industry by workers engaged, for that would be trustified caste control . . . the final control and destiny of the products of an industry must be in the hands of humanity as a whole. . . ."

Co-operation, he says, has been an attempt by the workers to get full control of their means of life and education. . . . Socialists have largely helped to develop the co-operative movement " from the conviction that by further knitting the workers together in the process of making and distributing commodities preparation is made for the ultimate control of all industries. . . . We intend to urge that the co-operative movement should supply jobs to workers victimised for their fight against the capitalists ; that a portion of its funds should be used to help in the social and political struggle against capitalism and that world co-operation should be established to bind the workers of all races more firmly together."

As to the socialist movement, " in view of the mighty forces the various States have summoned to their aid in the struggle of the nationally organised capitalists, it is sheer blind madness to talk of the uselessness of the State and of politics. . . . As socialists, we contend that the workers can use their existing and rapidly expanding State machinery for the fundamental re-organising and unifying of the whole of the processes of production and exchange and, he urges, " We, therefore, shall advocate the getting of the votes for all adults, the full democratisation of all public machinery of government, and the united use of the vote by the workers for the capture of all public bodies towards the attainment of the grand goal of a World Co-operative Industrial Democracy."

He concludes : " We do not think national wars are of benefit to the workers so we shall oppose all national wars as we oppose this one. *The only war that is worth waging is the Class War*, the workers against the world exploiters, until we have obtained industrial freedom."

Maclean had been given a hint that the authorities are about to take action against him. In a letter to Hugh Hinshelwood, dated 17th October, 1915, he writes among other matters : " Rosslyn Mitchell told Joe Maxwell (' Forward ' banner) that a writ was out against me under the Defence of the Realm Act. From a veiled hint in the ' Herald ' this week it looks as if the Glasgow authorities will take action against a few of us as soon as the Clyde trouble is over." John anticipates that the Govan School Board are about to dismiss him and then :

" The police will weigh in and seize me to justify their dismissal."

" My plans are prepared," he goes on. " We have a Free Speech Committee established as well as the Shop Stewards organisation. Take note, I would like you to be ready to get a Free Speech Committee formed in Greenock and take steps for my release, if I am arrested and jailed. Remember the police have been shorthanding my speeches all along and I am constantly shadowed. On Friday week two police and three 'tecs were at Mearns. Everyone knew the plain clothes men as absolute strangers. One shorthanded my speech. I stopped in my lecture and drew attention to it. It created a great sensation and will go the rounds as we desire. So please don't take my suggestions too lightly, for if we are well prepared we stave off opposition—meantime we are printing the notes of the Economic Class and selling them at a halfpenny a time. Perhaps you might get a study circle formed in Greenock or Gourock, and through the notes you could act as class leader. If the police seize me it would be good tactics to get the notes round as far as possible, and thus arouse interest in the subject. That will defeat the police aims.

" Yours frat.,

J. MACLEAN."

He had not long to wait. It was in the course of his meetings on 29th August and 2nd September that the first open clash between the authorities and John Maclean took place. He had been carrying on an extensive campaign of meetings throughout the city, making Bath Street the rallying centre on Sunday evenings. There had been a rival meeting in progress in Bath Street, and when it terminated a large number of people attending it gathered round Maclean's meeting. There were some interruptions. One individual in particular kept nagging at Maclean and shouting, " Why don't you enlist ? " Maclean replied, " I have been enlisted for fifteen years in the socialist army, which is the only army worth fighting for. God damn all other armies ! " At another meeting in Langside he had referred to the war as " this murder business," upon which a drunken soldier insisted that Maclean had called him a murderer.

On Wednesday, 27th October, 1915, John Maclean was brought before the Summary Court in Glasgow, charged under the Defence of the Realm Act, with uttering statements calculated to prejudice recruiting, and remitted to the Sheriff. On 10th November he was brought before Sheriff Lee in the Glasgow Court and was defended by Mr. Cassels.

Long before the proceedings of the court were due to begin large crowds of workers, coming from the various workshops and yards on the Clyde, had assembled in sympathy with the prisoner. The court was soon packed to overflowing. The Sheriff and the Court Officials were overwhelmed by the sight of this large body of uninvited guests marching in to see justice done. For over ten minutes the opening of the case had to be suspended until the " Public " had entered and settled down. Never had a Sheriff in Glasgow court had such an audience. Here in its sacred precincts in the gallery were to be found in their working attire, engineers, smiths, boilermakers, sheet-iron workers, labourers, etc.—the elite of the industrial working class, eager to watch proceedings which they felt were of tremendous importance for the whole labour movement.

The formalities of the opening over and the indictment read, the first brush between the defence and the prosecution took place following remarks of the Procurator-Fiscal. Breaking through all legal formalism Maclean, who was sitting like a lion in a cage eager to pounce at his enemies, ejaculated : " Do you want me to repeat again what I said at the meeting. I have been enlisted for fifteen years in the socialist army which is the only army worth fighting for ; God damn all other armies ! I have already said so, haven't I ? Did you not hear me ? " The audience gave vent to their feelings by stamping of feet and suppressed laughter at the discomfiture of the Procurator-Fiscal.

The Sheriff threatened to clear the court, but the spectators troubled little about formalities. They were enjoying the aggressiveness of Maclean and the defence.

The Prosecution relied for its witnesses upon four police detectives who had attended Maclean's meetings for the purpose of taking notes. Sixteen civilian witnesses on behalf of the Prosecution were in attendance at the court, but they were not called. With gramophonic monotony the police witnesses were kept repeating " God damn all armies," " God damn all armies," " God damn the army," " God damn all other armies," the only words they could remember when questioned by the defending counsel to show the confusion and unreliability of their testimony.

Finally, Maclean took the witness stand. He began his statement by saying that the words he used were : " I have enlisted in the socialist army fifteen years ago, the only army worth fighting for ; God damn all other armies," and added, " Take out of that what meaning you like."

Referring to a speech at the Langside Meeting, which had been quoted to show that he had tried to injure the feelings of soldiers, he said : " The major portion of the army is drawn from the working class, and I certainly did not say that soldiers were murderers. The soldiers belonging to the working class will not get any benefit from this war. I say here and now that the soldiers themselves are not murderers, but those who sent them and are sending them to the war are murderers."

In the course of the examination two incidents arose worth recording here.

The counsel for the defence demanded to know from the Police witnesses, who had heard the words spoken and complained of, why they did not inform the speaker at once that he was committing an offence, instead of prejudicing him by waiting for a month. The police reply was, " Our interference would have resulted in a riot."

In the second case, the Sheriff had asked the police witness, " What was the size of the audience at the time ? " " About three hundred," was the reply. " You mean to say," demanded the Sheriff, " that three hundred citizens of Glasgow heard a man say, ' God damn the King's army,' and did not resent it ? " " No one spoke," replied the detective.

In summing up the Sheriff took the opportunity to refer to the particular hardships of the Defence of the Realm Act. He said : " We certainly are dealing here with a very exceptional piece of legislation. This is not the ordinary law of the land, and in some ways is in opposition to the ordinary law. Of course, this particular legislation is an interference with the liberty of the subject, but there is no question, I think, at all that in these times of war the liberty of the subject has been interfered with over and over again, and in many different ways. Only the other day it was said that the result of the war had been to destroy, for the time being in the country, the liberty of conduct, the liberty of speech, and even the liberty of thought. All, however, that we have to deal with in this case is the liberty of speech. I wish to say this, however, because I think it is important. I asked a selection of the witnesses what the general impression of the audience was, and I asked questions to try and find out what the general line of the accused's speeches was. Now the accused makes no bones about this, that he is a person who holds very advanced political views and opinions. Holding these views it will be difficult for him to so choose his words, and so express himself, as not to give offence. He has been making speeches over a long period, and so far as I can gather we have only got these two offences libelled against him. Only on these two occasions had he allowed himself to slip. I think on one of the occasions there was a certain amount of provocation in respect that a person interfered with the meeting in what many might consider an irrelevant and impertinent way. On neither occasion did the accused seek to prosecute or elaborate upon what he had probably said on the spur of the moment."

As soon as the Sheriff had concluded his remarks and announced the sentence of £5 or five days imprisonment, shouts went up in the Court for " Three Cheers for Maclean ! " " Three Cheers for the Revolution ! " which were rendered lustily, followed by the singing of the Red Flag, as the crowd drifted from the Court. Maclean elected to go to prison rather than pay the fine.

The Prosecution of John Maclean was the signal for the starting of a permanent Free Speech Defence Committee. The first appeal issued in the name of the Committee was signed by Arthur McManus, as President.* It referred to the arrest of Maclean and went on to declare : " Under the cloak of the Defence of the Realm Act, the Government of Marconi-Ulster fame is deliberately destroying the elementary political rights of the people. In muzzling the working class they mean to destroy trade unionism. The fight against Maclean is a conspiracy against the working class. If we complacently allow this and similar prosecutions to take their course, if we permit the Government and the capitalists to pick out and intern the most active members of the Labour movement, we will be assisting in the destruction of the only valuable weapons the working class possesses. . . . In Glasgow we mean to contest them every inch of the way. A permanent Free Speech Committee has been formed, and already has affiliated Glasgow Trades Council, Govan Trades Council, Scottish Brassmoulders' Union, Almagamated Society of Engineers, Municipal Employees' Association, Dyers' Association, I.L.P., B.S.P., S.L.P., Scottish Prohibitionist Society, etc., etc."

" This is a hint to other districts to get a move on. Get your permanent Committee and form a means of establishing communications with each other, in order that we may let the

* Arthur McManus was an active shop steward and chairman of the National Committee of the Shop Stewards' Movement during the war. He took an active part in the formation of the Communist Party of Great Britain and was its first chairman, and was a member of the Central Committee until he died in 1927.

authorities see that there are still sufficient workers left to hold on to that which was won by the blood of their forefathers."

The conviction of Maclean was immediately followed up by his dismissal from his post as teacher. On the 16th November, the Govan Board of Education met to deliberate. A large crowd, mainly from the Govan District, had assembled outside the offices of the Board. The moment the doors were opened the Board-room was invaded, leaving outside a crowd of a thousand who kept up a chorus of revolutionary songs and cheer after cheer for Maclean.

The chairman and reactionary members of the Board deliberated in an ante-room as to whether the Board should meet behind closed doors. Harry Hopkins, District Secretary of the Amalgamated Society of Engineers, who was the one working class member of the Board, put up a strong fight for a public meeting. He was supported by Mr. Stewart, a co-operator, but it was decided by 9 votes to 2 to hold the meeting in private.

When the result of this vote became known, the electors present made a vigorous protest, hissing and booing the Chairman and the Board. The Chairman called upon the electors to leave the room. This they emphatically declined to do, and began singing the " Red Flag." Eventually on the appeal of Harry Hopkins, the crowd left the room.

But as one crowd left another kept surging in. Around the rostrum of the steps of the Board Offices a solid crowd listened for three hours to speeches on John Maclean and his educational activities on behalf of the working class.

Finally, when Hopkins appeared, and intimated that the Board, sitting in private, had by a large majority dismissed John Maclean, groans were shouted at the School Board and cheers given for Maclean. Singing the " Red Flag " and the " International " as they went, the crowd formed into line and marched down to the favourite meeting place in Bath Street, where further speeches were delivered.

The imprisonment and dismissal of John Maclean from his employment created great indignation throughout the whole labour movement in Glasgow. Hundreds of resolutions, protesting and demanding the reinstatement of Maclean, came in to the Free Speech Committee from all quarters. Suggestions went out for the Kinning Park and Plantation workers to withdraw their children from the Govan Board. At numerous meetings the demand was made for strike action. The workers in G. & W. Weir's, Cathcart, passed a resolution :

"That we immediately get into touch with all Conveners of Shop Stewards or Representatives of the Kindred Trades with a view to levying ourselves 1d., 2d., or such sum as would be sufficient to employ our victimised fellow-worker, John Maclean, as an independent organiser, at a salary equivalent to what he was in receipt of from the Govan School Board. Furthermore, that we henceforth labour unceasingly until Comrade Maclean is reinstated in his former position."

The day John Maclean was due to be released from Duke Street prison crowds of people gathered outside the prison gates at 7.45 a.m. to greet him. To avoid any demonstration the authorities had let him out a little before the usual time. A demonstration, however, did take place, a spectacular one at that. A deputation of forty miners in their working clothes, and with lamps burning, arrived from South Lanark in the Central Station, Glasgow, at nine o'clock. Marching through the streets this picturesque deputation caused a sensation in the city. On learning that Maclean was already released they marched out to Pollokshaws to make sure that their friend and comrade was really free and well. Then they marched through the town to a hall where a meeting was held. At one o'clock the deputation, with their lamps still burning, came to the gates of Fairfield shipyard, and a monster meeting of the workers was held.

A strong resolution of protest against the action of the Govan School Board was passed. Resolutions were also passed against the Munitions Act and Conscription. The crowd enthusiastically sang the "Red Flag" and the "International." Then the deputation went home, carrying the greetings of the shipyard to the miners in South Lanark.

In contrast to these manifestations of comradeship with Maclean was the attitude of the official leadership of the British Socialist Party. The day after the trial a letter of repudiation of Maclean was sent to the "Manchester Guardian," and signed by Dan Irving, " as an old member of the Party, a

member of the National Executive Committee and a Representative of the International Socialist Bureau."

Commenting on this letter and the hostile attitude of
" Justice," the official organ of the B.S.P., the " Vanguard "
for December 1915 wrote : " When Maclean stated that not
the soldiers were murderers, but those who sent them to war,
he undoubtedly was aware that within the B.S.P. were some
very active recruiting agents. We believe, however, that these
gentlemen should have long ago left the Party, and joined the
Conservatives." " So far as ' Justice ' is concerned it has long
been the echo of the ' Daily Express ' and the ' Morning
Post.' "

The clash between the Hyndman group of chauvinists and
the B.S.P. was heading for a split. And this took place at the
Annual Conference held in May 1916 in Salford, Manchester.
A recommendation from the Executive Committee to hold the
proceedings in camera and thus secure free discussion for the
delegates under the Defence of the Realm Act was opposed by
the Hyndman group. An amendment was proposed that only
the war policy discussion should be held in private. This was
defeated by 73 votes to 10. The vote for complete secrecy for
the whole proceedings was carried by 76 votes to 28. Amidst
uproar the minority withdrew from the Conference.

Hyndman and his supporters met afterwards in the Deans-
gate Hotel, Manchester, to review the situation and to issue a
statement. Subsequently, in June 1915, a preliminary Conference took place in London and the National Socialist Party
was formed, with Hyndman including such old S.D.F.'ers as
A. S. Headingley, H. W. Lee, Dan Irving, John Stokes, Will
Thorne, Jack Jones.

The letter of Dan Irving to the " Manchester Guardian "
referred to above and the reply leaves no doubt as to where
Maclean stood on the question of the war.

CHAPTER 8

THE RENT STRIKE MOVEMENT

SINCE the beginning of the war the house owners in Govan, Partick, Govanhill, Parkhead, Dennistoun and elsewhere in Glasgow had increased rents by as much as £1 to £3 per annum. In some cases a second increase was being demanded. The women refused to pay the increases and began forming committees under the auspices of the Women's Housing Council. A victory for the Govan Tenants gave a great impulse to the agitation, which soon manifested itself in the housewives on the Partick side of the river rough-handling the factors when they called for the rent.

A great demonstration converged on St. Enoch's Square, where speeches were made. From there the women marched to George Square, where delegates appealed to the Town Council to intervene on their behalf. The Council refused to discuss the matter, but the agitation and feeling was such that the Government was forced to intervene. It appointed a Commission of Enquiry—Dr. Hunter and Professor Scott—to deliberate on the matter. As soon as the factors heard the decision of the Government they immediately gave notice of rent increases all round, presumably to prepare a case for the Committee of Enquiry.

Numerous meetings were taking place all over the city when, the day following the decision to dismiss John Maclean from his employment by the Govan School Board, 17th November, eighteen munition workers were summoned before the Small Debt Court for refusing to pay increased rents. Several of the large shipyards in Govan—Harland and Wolff's, Stephens and Fairfield—as well as some on the other side of the river, struck work and marched in procession to the city. One contingent marched to Lorne Street School, took Maclean out and carried him shoulder high through the streets of Glasgow. He never returned to school again.

About ten thousand workers were estimated to be in the vicinity of the County Buildings. Standing on an improvised platform raised upon the shoulders of some comrades, the huge crowd was addressed by Maclean. The meeting resolved that unless the government took action to reduce rents to their pre-war level a general strike on the Clyde would follow. Another resolution was passed denouncing the action of the Govan School Board in dismissing John Maclean and demanding his reinstatement.

A large staff of police was stationed at the entrance to the Court, but they were unable to prevent a crowd from entering the buildings. A deputation from the workers outside was allowed to enter. Considerable delay ensued in opening the Court proceedings, and the crowd were getting impatient. Eventually Councillor Izett approached the Bar of the Court demanding, " Who is responsible for this Court ? " He was informed that the Sheriff was engaged elsewhere on another case. (There is every probability, as Gallacher says in his " Revolt on the Clyde," that he was in touch with the Government at that moment seeking advice on how to act in such an awkward situation.) " In the name of the workers I protest against this delay." The cheering that greeted this declaration of Councillor Izett brought the Sheriff from his chambers. Turning to the gallery he said they were permitted in the Court by his special sanction as they were legitimately interested in the proceedings that were to take place. Should there be any repetition of the noise, the Court would be cleared at once.

Mr. Malcolm Nimmo, one of the defenders, asked if the Sheriff would receive a deputation from the Dalmuir workers. After some hesitation the Sheriff pointed out that his position was purely a legal one, and that he had no authority to mix himself up with political questions. But these were exceptional times, and if he thought it would effect the desired purpose he was prepared to take the risk of receiving a deputation.

The deputation thereupon interviewed the Sheriff in his chambers.

The first spokesman said : " My Lord, I stand here as one of the deputation from Dalmuir shipbuilding yard, where over 8,000 workers are employed. When these men became aware of the fact that 18 tenants had been notified to appear before you to-day at this Court for refusing to pay an increase on their rent, they were on the point of stopping work to attend here ;

but they were advised to stay at their work and send a deputation. After discussion, they agreed to stay at work and send a deputation. The men are working under protest, and in the event of your deciding against the tenants they are determined to stop work. But should you decide in favour of the tenants these men are prepared to do all that lies in their power to assist the Government at this particular time. You know, my Lord, that the interests of the country are at stake, and it is your duty to assist the Government and the people of this country. The only way you can do that is by deciding in favour of the tenants. The country cannot do without these 8,000 workers, but the country can do without the factors. My Lord, I am of the opinion that the factors ought to be arrested and charged under the Defence of the Realm Act, as they have done more to injure recruiting than any one in Scotland that I know of. Mr. McKinnon Wood, Mr. Lloyd George and Mr. Hunter have suggested to the factors that they should stay their hand in the meantime."

The second speaker said he represented an engine shop, one of the principal shops on the Clyde. The decision of the men was to down tools and go to the Court in a body as a protest against the factors. But after discussion, they agreed, by a small majority, to send a deputation. The men were red hot, and the only way to avoid trouble was to have the cases dropped. He said that the workmen were prevented from leaving their particular work to go and better their positions, but the factor, who was under no Munitions Act, came along and raised the rents of those workmen. That was the actual position.

A representative from Dalmuir then read the following resolution : " That we, the organised workers of Beardmore's Naval Construction Works, Dalmuir, recognising that we are by Act of Parliament prevented from using this most propitious time to raise our wages, are determined to do all that lies in our power, even to the extent of downing tools, to prevent the landlords using the present extraordinary demand for houses to raise rents."

The Sheriff said he could not go into political questions. He was trying to see whether by continuation he could put off a decision that might give offence and trouble outside. There might be new laws by another week, and he should have thought that if it were possible it would be better not to force a decision ; but that was all he could do for them.

" You know the unfortunate position I am in. I never made the law ; my duty is to administer the law. This question has risen since the war started. Parliament is considering the question. Why not favour a continuation of the case ? "

A worker : " My Lord, I realise the unfortunate position you are in. You did not make the laws ; your duty is to administer them. But don't forget the fact that these laws were made in normal times, when everyone was living in peace. These are abnormal times. This is the time to make sacrifices. Who had a greater right than those who have everything to lose by a German invasion ? You hear the voice of the people out in the street. That is the workers of the upper reaches of the Clyde. These men will only resume work in the event of your deciding against the factor ; if you do not, it means that the workers on the lower reaches will stop work to-morrow and join them."

" Another worker said : " With all due respect, this talk about expiring laws reminds one of the bird in the hand being worth two in the bush. They were determined to keep hold of the bird, and were not going to consider any possible legislation. The workmen must have a decision to-day."

The Sheriff : " No doubt the rich people would say just the opposite. Every class has got its complaints. But that is going into political questions, which we cannot do here. At the present moment the Government is, as I understand, considering very seriously what is to be done as to the matter of rents, and I suppose everybody is agreed that some increase is absolutely justifiable. Everybody is also agreed that some greedy persons have made exorbitant demands on their tenants. One hopes it is a minority. The question is under consideration of the Government, and one hopes with confidence that a just decision will be come to very soon."

A worker : " That is why we want a decision to-day. We have left our work and are determined not to go back unless you give a decision in favour of the tenant. It might look like coercion, and we are sorry, but we are anxious to avoid serious trouble. If you decide in favour of the tenants, it will be an indication to the Government to move in our avour."

The Sheriff : " Alas ! alas ! it is not my decision which will be an indication to the Government ; it will be that horrible thought of industrial strife bringing untold misery into our midst."

A worker reminded the Sheriff that the deputation had no power to stop a strike. They could only tell the workmen the decision of the Court, and leave it to them. There would undoubtedly be a stoppage of work.

The Sheriff : " We have really gone into political matters, and we have failed to come to any suggestion of anything I can do to assist the matter. No one here would suggest an unjust decision. There has been no suggestion that any delay, that any joint conference between you and the factors might serve. We have tried our best, but I do not think we have done anything of the least public interest.

The Sheriff then adjourned to the Court.

When the Sheriff appeared on the bench the proceedings were short and sweet. All the cases were dropped. A cheer was given for the Sheriff and the demonstrators joyfully marched home.

The first Rent Restrictions Act was hurriedly passed by the Government.

Commenting on this strike movement " The Vanguard " for December carried a leading article in which we have no doubt is to be found a faithful reflection of Maclean's views and the standpoint which guided him in all his activities up to his untimely death. For these reasons we excuse ourselves for quoting it at length. It declares : " It should be noted that the rent strike on the Clyde is the first step towards the political strike so frequently resorted to on the continent in times past. We rest assured that our comrades in the various works will incessantly urge this aspect on their shopmates, and so prepare the ground for the next great countermove of our class in the raging class warfare—raging more than ever during the Great Unrest period of three or four years ago."

After adding a note of warning to be prepared for future struggles, the article goes on to say : " Whether the Clyde Workers' Committee as constituted to-day is able or willing to cope with the situation is doubtful, but it is just as well to give it a further chance with the added support of miners and railwaymen. However, just as this unofficial committee views with suspicion the official committees of the various unions, and attempts to act as a driving force, we warn our comrades that they ought to adopt the same attitude towards the unofficial committee and see that it pushes ahead. If it still clings on to academic discussions and futile proposals it is their business to take the initiative into their own hands as they did on the recent rent strike. Remember that the only way to fight the class war is by accepting every challenge of the master class and throwing down more challenges ourselves. Every determined fight binds the workers together more and more and so prepares for the final conflict . . . to the end of establishing socialism."

It is to be noted here that attention is drawn, and rightly so, to the importance of the political strike. Only the political strike is seen as the culmination of a spontaneous mass movement " that would engage in the final conflict . . . to the end of establishing socialism." The " comrades " by which term Maclean is here referring to the active militant workers, are warned to stand guard and be critical of the unofficial movement equally with the official trade union organisations. But it is noticeable there is a complete absence of any reference to party leadership, or to the role of the party in the establishment of socialism. This is an example of the big weakness to be shown in the whole of the movement on the Clyde during the war, where the importance of the party was subordinated to the spontaneous mass movement.

CHAPTER 9

THE THREE TRIALS IN 1916

As already mentioned in Chapter 6 there had been many flagrant violations of the ministerial pledge given to the Labour Members of Parliament that Munition Courts would not imprison workmen. The three shipwrights who were victims in the Fairfield case were still in prison. Dissatisfaction with the Government's policy towards labour was manifest and widespread. The Government took the course of sending to Glasgow a Commission to investigate the situation and to report. The Commissioners were Sir George Askwith, who was then Chief Industrial Commissioner, and Isaac Mitchell, a former official of the Amalgamated Society of Engineers, but now in the service of the Government. The Commission appeared to be influenced by what they learned in the course of their investigations, and recommended an immediate enquiry into the grievances of the workmen against the Munitions Act.

Without delay the Government appointed Lord Balfour of Burleigh and Sir Linden Macassey as a Commission of Enquiry. The Commission held its sittings in the Central Hotel, Glasgow. Balfour tried to ingratiate himself into the graces of all concerned by always speaking the " Doric " and giving the impression he was one of " theirs." In the course of its proceedings the Commission made a special visit to Duke Street Prison, where the three shipwrights lay, in order to take their evidence. Its main recommendation to the government was the necessity to revise the policy of imprisonment.

In the meantime the Clyde Workers' Committee was up in arms against what was in practice bringing the workers under military law. For generations the trade unionists and socialists had resisted any suggestion of compulsion and interference with their traditional independent liberties, and here surely was a challenge they felt bound to accept. A big campaign was opened demanding the withdrawal of this order, and a special manifesto was issued in 150,000 copies.

It is no part of our purpose here to retell the story of the St. Andrew's Hall meeting on 25th December, 1915, and Mr. Lloyd George's visit to the Clyde, or of the suppression of the " Forward " and " Vanguard," which latter, the paper of John Maclean, was declared by Lloyd George to be the most violent of any in Glasgow. That story has been adequately dealt with by Wm. Gallacher, M.P., in " Revolt on the Clyde," and in the present author's " Pioneering Days." *

We would merely record here that when the St. Andrew's Hall meeting broke up a big procession was formed outside,

* For a concise account and summary of the story of the attack on the press, see " The New Statesman " for that month (January 1915).

which marched through the principal streets to Glasgow Green, where a meeting was addressed by Harry Hopkins, District Secretary of the Amalgamated Society of Engineers, Tom Clark, John Maclean, Arthur McaManus, John W. Muir, leading shop steward and Councillor John Wheatley, who was later to become Minister of Health in the Labour Government.

At the first session of Parliament in 1916 an amending act to the Munitions of War Act was introduced, to do away with the penalty of imprisonment, and in this respect the Government responded to the recommendations of its Commissioners. But while it appeared the Government had ceded, as a matter of fact Lloyd George had up his sleeve an " Order in Council " prepared days before the debate began. He never mentioned this to the Labour leaders or trade unionists who had been pressing him on the need for revision of the Act. By this " Order in Council " it became for the first time a criminal act under the Defence of the Realm Act, punishable by imprisonment with hard labour, for any person to impede, delay, or restrict the production, repair or transport of raw materials, or any other work necessary for the successful prosecution of the war. By a special provision of the Order, the Minister of Munitions was given concurrent powers of prosecution with the competent military authority. Offences might, if thought fit, be tried by Court Martial and in camera. Thus the net was cast wide enough to bring in anyone who might be considered troublesome to the Government.

John Maclean, as we have seen, was extremely active prior to his arrest. Following his release from imprisonment he had been addressing workgate meetings during the day and public meetings in the evenings, denouncing the war, the government and conscription. He was the first victim of the new powers of the Government. On 1st February, 1916, he was arrested and handed over to the military authorities in Edinburgh Castle. But the public pressure was such that the military authorities were obliged to release him and hand him back to the Civic magistrates. Maclean appeared in private before the Sheriff, who released him on Monday, 14th February, on bail of a £100, to come up for trial in April.

The Government were evidently bent on crushing the revolt on the Clyde. A special dilution Commission was sent to

Glasgow. The Clyde Workers' Committee tried to get the different shops to meet the Commissioners but to refer all questions to the Committee before agreement. In this they were not successful. Independent agreements were entered into by several shops with the managements.

It was rising out of the interpretation of the independent agreement come to between Parkhead Forge workers and the management, that the Convener of Shop Stewards, David Kirkwood, now M.P., was prevented from going from one department to another in the course of his duties as steward. On Friday, 17th March, 1916, the men stopped work. Eight days afterwards, in the early hours of Saturday morning, 25th March, five of the Parkhead Shop Stewards were arrested : Kirkwood, Shields, Haggerty, Wainwright and Faulds. Arthur MacManus and James Messer, who were stewards in J. and J. Weir's, Cathcart, were also arrested the same morning. The latter two arrests arose out of protests and complaints of a flagrant violation of the agreement arrived at between the Dilution Committee of Weir's and the Commissioners.

Following a mass meeting of the Cathcart workers, held on a Sunday, the decision was taken by a small majority to down tools as a protest against the arrest of their stewards. In view, however, of the smallness of the majority another meeting was called on the Monday. Inconclusive discussion went on, and further meetings took place on Tuesday. On Wednesday morning, 29th March, Harry Glass, Bridges and Kennedy, shop steward's in Weirs', were arrested. To these were added Tom Clark. The policy of the Government in getting separate agreements signed undoubtedly prevented unity of action and organised resistance, and for a period the ferment died down.

John Maclean under remand and the leading shop stewards out of the way, the Government next turned its attention to the Clyde Workers' Committee and its paper, " The Worker." In the March issue of " The Worker " there appeared an unsigned article, entitled " Should the Workers Arm ?—A Desperate Situation." The paper was confiscated, and the editor, John W. Muir, then a member of the S.L.P., William Gallacher, Chairman of the Clyde Workers' Committee, and a member of the B.S.P., and Walter Bell, a member of the S.L.P.

and Business Manager of the Socialist Labour Press, printers, were arrested and remanded for trial.

Next came the arrest of the colleague of John Maclean, James D. MacDougall, of James Maxton, subsequently the M.P. for Bridgeton Division, and of Jack Smith, an associate of a small group of intellectual anarchists in Glasgow. On the day following the deportations of the shop stewards, Sunday, 26th March, a large protest meeting had taken place on Glasgow Green. At this meeting the three last-named accused men had made speeches denouncing the Government and military compulsion and calling for a general strike.

The proceedings at the High Court in Edinburgh (where the three separate trials—of John Maclean, of Muir, Gallacher and Walter Bell, and of Maxton, MacDougall and Smith—took place) throws an interesting sidelight, on the one hand upon the resolution of the Government faced with mass unrest and on the other hand upon the leadership of the workers' movement, unofficial and official, whose irresolution was in marked contrast to the determination and vindictiveness of the Government.

The first of the trials, that of John Maclean, began on 11th April, 1916, before the Lord Justice-General (Lord Strathclyde). The Prosecution was led by Mr. Robert Munro, the Lord Advocate, assisted by his deputy. Maclean was defended by Mr. MacRobert and Mr. Alexander P. Duffes, later a Scottish K.C.

There were six counts in the indictment against Maclean, each concerning statements alleged to have been made at separate meetings during the month of January 1916.

Summarised, these were that he had declared that :

(1) conscription was unnecessary, as the Government had plenty of soldiers and munitions ; that after the war conscription would be used to secure cheap labour ; that should the Government enforce the Military Service Act and Munitions Act the workers should " down tools " ; that if the British soldiers laid down their arms the Germans would do the same, as all were tired of the War ;

(2) the workers should strike in order to attend a meeting ;

(3) the workers should " down tools " and resist conscription ;

(4) if conscription became law the workers would become conscripts to industrial labour ; the real aim of the Government ;

(5) the workers should strike and those who had guns should use them ;

(6) the workers should sell or pawn their alarm clocks, sleep in in the morning and not go to work.

The plea was not guilty. For the Prosecution there were 18 witnesses, all policemen. For the Defence, all the witnesses aimed at disproving the charge of advocating " down tools " and strike action.

The central feature of the trial was the appearance of Maclean in the witness box. He refused to take the oath, and affirmed. He began with preliminary remarks to the effect that he was a socialist and a member of the B.S.P., but held no official position in that party. He was closely associated with the efforts made for the better housing of the workers, as Secretary of the National Housing Association, to which, he remarked, no honorarium was attached.

Taken over the counts in the indictment by his counsel, he said he was against conscription absolutely. He had not said anything at the meetings in question about downing tools or striking. At a meeting he had been asked whether the laying down of arms by either side would end the war, and he had said, offhand, yes ; but thought it was utopian. It was ridiculous to charge him with having advised the workers to use guns ; the workers have no guns.

Under cross-examination by the Lord Advocate, he said he had been devoting his time to the most important thing in the world—the establishment of a Labour College. He began a class for conscientious objectors. There was a class on trade unionism. He was a socialist and not a syndicalist. He had been a socialist for fifteen years, lived all his life in Glasgow, and had been speaking lately almost every day on the Labour College.

The Lord Advocate suggested that Maclean's purpose was to provoke a strike in order to compel the Government to withdraw the Conscription Bill. "That is not so," replied Maclean. "I have spoken on conscription at Beardmore's and Weir's, but that was to explain the dangers of it. I favour demonstration as a method of resisting conscription."

Yes, he declared, in answer to a further question, he was in favour of strikes. "At this particular juncture in the nation's affairs?" pressed the Lord Advocate. "That depends," was the cautious reply. "One was against strikes at this juncture so far as munition workers are concerned. It was quite legal for other workers to strike."

Asked if he had never on any occasion advised munition workers to strike, he replied, "Yes, I did." When the workers at a meeting passed a resolution giving the Government a week to make up its mind on the question of rent, he had gone round advising the workers to stand by the men who passed the resolution.

He insisted that, determined at all costs to obtain a conviction, the policemen, since he said nothing about "downing tools," had charged him with something he did not say. He referred to his visit to Weir's gates where, as he had been told, the clerks telephoned for the police immediately he arrived. Maclean agreed he had never made a speech in favour of recruiting. He had made none against it. Let every man choose for himself, he argued.

Summing up for the jury, Lord Strathclyde said that undoubtedly there was a conflict of evidence, but there was evidence for the Crown to support the charges libelled. But, he pointed out, *a verdict against the Crown would involve a charge of conspiracy against the police.* (Italics ours.) He next dealt with the gravity of the charges at this juncture and said, if an offence were committed against these regulations, then he must regard it as a felony, and the punishment for a felony might be penal servitude for life.

With such a charge to the Jury it was clear that the Government meant business. For Maclean the die was cast. One hour and five minutes later the Jury pronounced Maclean guilty on the first four charges, not proven on the fifth, and not guilty on the sixth.

Before passing sentence the Judge was very brief. He said to Maclean, "After a patient and long consideration and investigation you have been found guilty, not for the first time, of contravening the regulations of the Defence of the Realm Act.

" On a former occasion a very light sentence was passed upon you, with the intention, no doubt, of being a warning and acting as a deterrent. It seems to have failed. To a man so intelligent and highly educated as you appear to be, it would be idle for me to dwell upon the gravity of the offence of which the Jury have found you guilty. It is thoroughly well known to you, as it is to the whole community. The sentence of the court is that you be sent to penal servitude for a period of three years."

Maclean appeared to take the sentence very quietly, and was being moved from the dock, when from the gallery came cries of " Cheer up, John," at which Maclean waved his hat in reply. Thereupon the company in the gallery started to sing the " Red Flag " and an order was given to clear the court. In spite of this, however, the people continued singing as they filed out of the gallery.

For their part in this demonstration of solidarity with Maclean four men were arrested and the next day fined £2 or 14 days in prison.

The next trial was that of Muir, Gallacher and Walter Bell, on 13th April, 1916, in the same Court and before the same Judge and Prosecuting Counsel. The charge was that No. IV of " The Worker," dated 29th January, 1916, contained an article, " Should the Workers Arm ? " This article was alleged to be " Calculated and intended to cause sedition and dis-affection among the civil population of Glasgow and to impede, delay and restrict the production, repair and transport of war material thereby contravening the Defence of the Realm Act and Regulations." The accused were defended by Mr. Paton and Mr. Duffes.

In his " Revolt on the Clyde," Gallacher has given a critical appreciation of the weaknesses of the defence, above all of the lack of experience and guidance which allowed the character of the defence to be chiefly determined by professional lawyers.

Before passing sentence the Judge said that the article seemed to him in very plain and forcible language to tell the workers that physical force and violence was their last and only resort if the method of a universal strike failed to protect the

workers against the supposed attack made upon them through
the Munitions Act and Military Service Act and dilution of
Labour.

They had through the mouthpiece of their Counsel on Thursday expressed their regret for the publication of that article.
His Lordship was sorry that the regret was not expressed at an
earlier stage of the case, not expressed before the Jury had come
to consider their case, but was tendered only after the Jury had
come to the conclusion that the men had committed the offence

After returning a verdict of " Guilty," the Court was
adjourned until the following day, when Muir and Gallacher
were sentenced to twelve months' imprisonment, and Walter
Bell to three months.

Nearly one month later, on 11th May, 1916, James Maxton,
James D. MacDougall and Jack Smith appeared in the same
High Court at Edinburgh, before the same Judge and Lord
Advocate. They were defended by Alexander P. Duffes,
instructed by Rosslyn Mitchell, a Glasgow Labour Lawyer.

The indictment was that on Glasgow Green, on 26th March,
1916, at a meeting called to oppose the Military Service Act and
to protest against the deportation of the Shop Stewards in
Glasgow, MacDougall had advocated " Strike, strike, strike,
and to hell with them ! " Maxton was alleged to have declared,
" It was now for the workers to take action, and that action
was to strike and down tools at once." They were charged
under the same section of the Defence of the Realm Act and
Regulations, as Muir, Gallacher and Walter Bell.

For the Defence, Counsel endeavoured to show that the
accused " were not really unpatriotic." MacDougall had been
instrumental in getting his School Board to feed soldiers'
children. " They meant what they said at the time, but they
were induced to say it by the state of their feelings, and they
now regretted it. . . . They had been in prison for six weeks,
and they had asked him to express to his lordship their regret
at their quite inexcusable action on the occasion in question."*

But even this humiliating declaration did not help the de-
fendants. As William Gallacher with complete justice em-

*James Maxton—Portrait of a Rebel," by Gilbert McAllister.
Published by John Murray.

phasises in his book : " Capitulation simply played into
their hands. Weakness and timidity can avail us nothing in
such a situation." Each of them were sentenced to twelve
months to run concurrently from date of arrest. Jack Smith
got an extra six months for being in possession of certain
literature.

The behaviour of some responsible leaders of the Glasgow
Trades Council that year shows how deeply they were influenced by the war policy of the Government and that of the
official policy of the Labour Party. Following the deportations
the decision was taken by the Council to hold a demonstration
of protest on Sunday, 17th April, 1916. It was intended to
muster on George Square and march through the streets to
Glasgow Green. When the magistrates had the application
before them from George Carson, Secretary of the Trades
Council, it was rejected by 16 votes to 2.

A sub-committee of the Council considered the reply of the
Magistrates with a view to getting the decision rescinded. One
Magistrate hinted that the trouble was the public objections
against meetings in George Square, but if the demonstration
was confined to Glasgow Green it might be possible to get
consent.

William Shaw reported to the next full Council meeting that
" It was the unanimous decision of the Executive Committee to
accept the ruling of the sub-committee not to go on with the
demonstration. . . . Frankly he was not prepared to butt his
head against a stone wall. What happened to John Maclean
and others when they were arrested ? Why, the bulk of the
workers said they were damned fools."

An attempt to reject acceptance of the Executive's report
led to an uproar. The Chairman of the Council, G. Shanks,
declared " he was dead against ' down tools ' and all that
nonsense. . . . He counselled the Trades Council to have no
representation at a demonstration which had not the approval
of the magistrates."

Clearly with such a disposition the Trades Council leadership
was not likely to assist in any way to take up the challenge of
a Government striking at the spokesmen and the organisations
of the working class. Had it done so, and met it with a spirit of

defiance and working class dignity, the whole course of events in the Clyde might have taken a different turn.

The press seized the occasion of these trials to make scurrilous attacks on the prisoners, particularly on John Maclean. "The Greenock Telegraph" distinguished itself by a vindictive leading article, which drew from Hugh Hinshelwood the following letter in reply:

THE TRIAL OF JOHN MACLEAN

Gourock, 18th April, 1916.

Sir,—In to-day's issue of your paper you devote your leading article to the trial of John Maclean. In your endeavour to hold up to the reader the terrible menace to our liberties through Maclean and his work you overstep yourself when you say he battened on the workers. His services have been utilised in connection with various movements in the town. The national crusade against consumption was anticipated so far as Greenock was concerned quite three years previous by the Trades Council acting on the suggestion of Maclean. Likewise, the agitations which culminated in the Local Government Board inquiry into the inspection (?) of carcasses of the slaughterhouse, and only recently the same Board's inquiry into the housing conditions. All of the work done in connection with these was given without any thought of recompense. I gladly avail myself of this opportunity to clear Maclean of seeking to benefit himself. He has sacrificed his liberty through the same spirit that prompted him in the above laudable work. My averment regarding the part he took in the Housing Council's work can easily be ascertained from the several ministers of religion who were brought into contact with him at its inception.—Yours, etc.,

HUGH HINSHELWOOD.

To this letter the Editor appended the following note:

(What our correspondent alleges may or may not be true, but it makes little difference now what good Maclean has done in the past. He has been proved a traitor to his country at a time when it needs most help.)

F

CHAPTER 10

SOVIET CONSUL

WITH the arrests and repressive measures of the Government the agitation on the Clyde subsides until early in 1917, when it begins to raise its head again. On 3rd February Maxton was released, and MacDougall two days later. Ten days afterwards Muir and Gallacher came out of prison. A great reception was accorded to the ex-prisoners on 16th February in the St. Mungo Halls. In his speech Gallacher stirred the vast audience to the depths by a reference to " one missing that night, John Maclean." The thunderous applause marked the opening of a wide and popular campaign for Maclean's release.

Suddenly the news flashes across the wires, " Revolution in Russia ! " The whole labour movement becomes agog with excitement. " Yes, John Maclean was right. Revolution is bound to come. This is only the beginning." Such were the sentiments frequently to be heard in Glasgow. A great Conference is held in Leeds in support of the Russian Revolution, and to set up a Workers' and Soldiers' Council for Great Britain. In the projected Council for Scotland the name of Maclean is included.

At a meeting in St. Andrew's Hall, Glasgow, on 13th May, George Lansbury is prompted by the feeling among the audience to move a resolution demanding the release of Maclean. A " John Maclean Release Committee " is formed with Harry Hopkins, A.S.E., as Secretary, and a tremendous agitation is launched, in the course of which the Government is bombarded with telegrams and resolutions from organisations and personalities demanding Maclean's release.

The bourgeoisie in Glasgow was intent on wiping out the stigma on its honour that marked the reception given to Lloyd George in 1915. On 29th June, 1917, Lloyd George came north to receive the freedom of the City of Glasgow. The ceremony took place in St. Andrew's Hall. So dense and hostile was the crowd outside the hall, that fearing trouble, a cordon of soldiers and police were drawn up to keep the crowd back ; Maxton,

Kirkwood and Agnes Dollan were addressing the crowd, when a Red Flag was seen to flutter from a window opposite the Hall. A deputation later asked for a loan of the banner. Headed by this red banner several thousands, four abreast, marched through the streets to Duke Street Prison, where it was known John Maclean was lying. Gathering up against the main gateway the " Red Flag " was sung and cheers given for John Maclean. One adventurous enthusiast climbed up to the highest part of the wall and fixed the red banner. The next day, 30th June, John Maclean was released on ticket of leave, having served 14 months and 22 days of his three years' sentence.

Nobody in the ranks of the workers' movement believed that Lloyd George's visit to Glasgow had anything to do with the release of John Maclean. The release of Maclean was undoubtedly a tribute to the deep unrest and widespread agitation throughout the country, and to the influence of the Russian Revolution. Lenin had already acclaimed John Maclean for his fearless stand against the imperialist war. It was not surprising that the first All-Russian Congress of Workers' and Soldiers' Councils at Petrograd should send international greetings and appoint as honorary members of the presidium of the Congress John Maclean, with his comrade Karl Leibknecht, " those socialists," as Lenin said, " who put the idea of revolutionary struggle against imperialist war into life."

On Monday, 10th July, 1917, a great reception was given to Maclean in the St. Mungo Halls, presided over by Tom Johnston of " The Forward," later Secretary of State for Scotland. At this gathering Maclean referred to the bad treatment he had been given in Perth and Peterhead prisons. He repudiated any suggestion of benevolence or charitableness on the part of the Government, but attributed his release to the public agitation and to the Russian Revolution. A presentation was made to him from E. C. Fairchild, Chairman of the B.S.P. That same week Maclean was served with his military calling-up papers, but they were immediately cancelled.

With the Russian Revolution a new problem had arisen. The Government began to intern many of the Russians who had taken refuge in this country from the terror of Czarism.

There were hundreds of Poles, Lithuanians, and Letts in Lanarkshire, working in the mines and steel works.

Walking through some parts of Bellshill one might have imagined it to be a part of old Russia, judging from the names above the shops and the foreign dialect overheard in the streets. The deportation of the menfolks left a problem of relief for the dependents.

John Maclean threw himself heart and soul into this work. A Russian Political Refugee Committee was formed with Maclean as Chairman. Appeals were made for help and a campaign was begun for the release of the prisoners awaiting deportation. Notable amongst these was Chicherin, who was later deported and became world famous as the Soviet Commissar for Foreign Affairs.

Among those interned was a certain Peter Petrov. Petrov was one of the many foreign emigrants living in London. For a time he appears to have been engaged in research work for the Social Democratic Party of Germany, and moving in refugee circles he came in touch with British Social Democrats and was subsequently introduced to John Maclean.

Petrov had early taken up a hostile attitude to Hyndman and from the beginning of the war formed part of the anti-war group in the B.S.P. This, in addition to his vaunted knowledge of the international socialist movement and his revolutionary associations, no doubt enabled him to ingratiate himself with John Maclean, who brought him to Glasgow in 1915.

The estimation given by William Gallacher in his "Revolt on the Clyde," of Petrov's influence on Maclean is by no means an exaggeration. Revolutionary verbiage, conspiratorial romanticism, and a capacity for seeing police agents in every shadow was certainly not a healthy influence for such a temperament as John Maclean.

Simultaneously with his work Maclean was lecturing every week-end in "The International Hall," Stockwell Street, Glasgow, and travelling up and down the country insisting everywhere that we learn from the experiences of the Russain Revolution. At a time when the cry for peace by negotiation was becoming loudest in the camp of the I.L.P., the pacifists and some religious circles, Maclean was declaring, "I want peace, but it must be a peace with revolution in it."

In January 1918 he attended the famous Labour Party Conference at Manchester where Arthur Henderson received a severe trouncing from the left for his part in the Clydeside affairs, especially the deportation of the Shop Stewards. Maclean returned convinced of the need for carrying on a determined struggle against what he called the " Labour traitors " who had joined the Government to help wage the imperialist war.

On 1st February, 1918, he was highly honoured. He received a message from M. Litvinoff, who was the representative of the new Socialist Republics of Russia, though still unacknowledged by the British Government, appointing him Consul for Soviet Affairs in Great Britain. This was an arduous post for one who was not even a subject of the country concerned, and likely to involve further persecution. But this could not deter Maclean from what he regarded as his revolutionary obligation. He opened an office for the Consulate, 12 Portland Street, Glasgow.

He immediately occupied himself with the protection and defence of the interests of the Russian nationals interned. He took part in the organisation of an International Women's Protection League, and opened a Fund on their behalf, of which he was appointed Treasurer.

But he was handicapped on all sides by the police and authorities, whose class hatred would not allow them to recognise either Consulate or Consul. All correspondence addressed to the Consulate was returned to the senders marked

> " Such Consul not recognised by His Majesty's Government."

Once more the police were on his track. On Friday afternoon, 22nd March, 1918, two detectives raided the Consulate and arrested Louis Shamus, Maclean's assistant. Shamus was removed to Barlinnie Prison to await deportation. On Monday afternoon, 13th April, 1918, two detectives again raided the Consulate ; Maclean himself was arrested, charged with sedition. This was to prove the greatest trial of his career and to rank as one of the great political trials in Scottish history.

CHAPTER 11

THE 1918 TRIAL : MACLEAN ACCUSES

THE trial opened before Lord Strathclyde, the Lord Justice
General, and a jury at the High Court at Edinburgh on Thursday, 9th May, 1918. Out of their great interest in the case, and
in token of their solidarity, a large number of workers left
Glasgow the day before the trial and marched to Edinburgh to
give Maclean their moral support. This meant marching all
night. Unfortunately, before they arrived the Court was
packed with Edinburgh people, including of course, plain
clothes policemen.

There were eleven charges in the indictment, which accused
Maclean of addressing audiences in Glasgow, Shettleston,
Cambuslang, Lochgelly and Harthill, consisting in part of the
civilian population, and in part of persons engaged in the production, repair, or transport of raw material, or in other work
necessary for the successful prosecution of the war, and making
statements which were likely to prejudice the recruiting,
training and discipline of H.M. Forces, and by which he further
attempted to cause mutiny, sedition, and disaffection among
the civilian population, and to impede, delay, or restrict the
production of war material, etc., contrary to the Defence of
the Realm Act.

The first speech was made on 20th January, and the last on
4th April. The statements charged against Maclean, and
which the indictment regarded as likely to have the effects
above described, were that " tools should be downed," the
" revolution should be created," " that the Clyde district had
helped to win the Russian Revolution," and that " the revolutionary spirit on the Clyde was at present ten times as strong
as it was two years ago " ; that " the workers on the Clyde
should take control of the City Chambers, and retain hostages
and take control of the Post Offices and the banks " ; that
" the farmers should be compelled to produce food for the
workers, and if they refused their farms should be burned " ;
that " the movement would be supported by the French

Canadians and the workers in New York " ; and that " other districts would follow the Clyde " ; that " the present House of Commons should be superseded by a Soviet, and he did not care whether they met in the usual place or in Buckingham Palace " ; and that " the workers in the munition works should be advised to restrict their output." It was alleged that on other occasions he advocated the seizing of newspaper offices, also the food stores on the Clyde and the ships—that he said the soldiers and sailors were with the workers, that " the workers should profit by the experience of their Russian brothers," and that " he was prepared to run any risk if he thought he could bring about a social revolution in Glasgow." This was quite a formidable indictment leaving no loophole for escape.

Maclean, who for the first time conducted his own case, refused to plead, and when the Lord Justice General intimated that he could object to any particular juryman, he replied, " I would object to the whole of them." There were no witnesses for the defence. Twenty-eight witnesses were examined for the prosecution, of whom twenty-three were police witnesses, eight being special constables, belonging— with the exception of two warehousemen and a compositor— to the professional class. Of the remaining five civilian witnesses, two were shorthand writers employed by the police, there was one newspaper reporter, a mining inspector, and a working man who followed the occupation of slater.

In cross-examining the witnesses Maclean pursues them not with the finesse of a trained Lawyer, but with the keen irresistible logic of the defender of his class. He counters the lying insinuations that German gold was circulating in the Clyde Workers' movement by revealing that the British Government had taken away a cheque for £1,000 from Kameneff, who had been sent from Soviet Russia to be its ambassador in Britain. " Quite a moral thing to do from a capitalist point of view," interjects Maclean, " and therefore, the Consul had been left without money and without means of support in Glasgow."

He pursues the police witnesses on the veracity of their " mental notes." Police-detectives were obliged to admit that their reports were written from memory after Maclean's meetings. Witness : " I was not afraid to take notes openly, but I did not think it judicious." Maclean : " You thought you should go there as a spy and not let the people know what you were ; that you were a spy ? " Witness : " Not necessarily." Maclean : " Spies are shot ! "

He exposes on the basis of government statistics that production had increased threefold, but that the workers' wages had not increased threefold. He attacks the Government for holding up the food supplies. He defends the Russian Revolution against the charge of violence, " the most peaceful revolution the world has ever seen, and it is the biggest," he declares.

In the spirit of Marx at the Cologne Trials and of the Bolsheviks in Russia, Maclean utilises the court as a tribune to speak to the masses of the people, to make a burning indictment of capitalism. He does not regard himself as the accused. " I am not here," he declares, " as the accused. I am here as the accuser of Capitalism, dripping with blood from head to foot." This ringing challenge echoes through the hallowed precincts of the stuffy bourgeois court, is re-echoed into the outer world, relayed from village to village, from town to town, wherever workers congregate, a fitting expression of the man, the socialist, the unflinching revolutionary.

The speech of Maclean is an historic document of great importance. Any attempt to summarise it or to make selections from it could not adequately convey to the reader the ideas, the criticisms, and revolutionary fervour of the man.

The speech must be read as a whole and in the light of the historic conditions leading up to and during the first world war, to be adequately understood. Suffice it to say Maclean takes up the charges levelled against him one by one ; his advocacy of " Ca' canny," the " down tools " policy, the seizure of food, the breaking up of the Harmsworth printing press ; his defence of women and children, especially the dependents of the Russian exiles who had been deported ; his opinions upon the attitude of the Allies to the Bolsheviks, Russia's fight for Freedom, and the Brest Litovsk negotiations ; the question of the Constitution and the rush for Empire.

He concludes : " I am a socialist, and have been fighting and will fight for an absolute reconstruction of Society for the benefit of all. . . . I act square and clean for my principles. I have nothing to retract. I have nothing to be ashamed of. . . . No matter what your accusations against me may be ; no matter what reservations you keep at the back of your head, my appeal is to the working class. . . . They and they only can bring about the time when the whole world will be one brother-hood, on a sound economic foundation."

The speeches finished, the Lord Justice General charged the Jury. Without retiring the Jury intimated through their foreman a verdict of guilty on all Charges. " Have you anything to say, John Maclean ? " asked the Judge. " No," replied Maclean, " I think I have said enough for one day."

It is significant that the Judge declined to make a long speech, saying it would be idle to do so, because, addressing Maclean, " You are obviously a highly educated and intelligent man and realise the thorough seriousness of the offence you have committed."

" To-day the sentence of the Court is that you be sent to penal servitude for a period of five years." Maclean, turning to the friends in the Court, shouted : " Keep it going, boys ; keep it going."

CHAPTER 12

HUNGER STRIKE : RELEASE

In the course of his speech in his defence Maclean had in-cidentally referred to the doctors in Peterhead prison. He alleged he was fevered up, when he was in prison, and then chilled down ; that potassium bromide was used to lower his temperature, to disturb the organs and nervous system. He cited references to the experience of the conscientious objectors in prison, and on the basis of his own previous experiences he declared : " This callous and cold system of destroying people is going on inside prisons now," and he gave notice that he would take no food inside prison. " If food is forcibly fed, then my friends have got to bear in mind that if any evil happens to me, I am not responsible for the consequences, but the British Government."

In this mood and with this determination he went to Perth prison en route for Peterhead penitentiary. The Scottish bourgeoisie smirked its smug satisfaction that this "damned bolshevik" was put out of the way. Unfortunately Maclean did not belong to any powerful trade union, or any well organised body capable of intimidating the Government. Protest meetings were held, and throughout the labour movement there was great indignation, but months passed before this indignation was crystallised into a movement inconvenient to the Government.

In the meantime Mrs. Maclean was receiving anonymous letters from certain women in the district where the Macleans lived, "referring to the brutal murders of the Bolshevik class that you belong to," and threatening to burn down her house if she did not leave the district soon. To add to her worries, there were grave rumours about John's health, and considerable anxiety as to his fate, in view of his public declaration at the trial not to eat prison food. An attempt had been made to send food into the prison, but the scheme fell through by reason of Maclean's firm determination to continue the hunger strike. Mrs. Maclean tried hard to get to see him, but to all her enquiries she received merely assurances that John was in the best of health. When at last she did see him she was shocked at "his aged and haggard appearance." Mrs. Maclean immediately wrote the following letter to the leader of the British Socialist Party, E. C. Fairchild, who printed it in "The Call." It was subsequently reproduced in "The Herald" and other papers :—

23rd October, 1918.

Dear Mr. Fairchild,

I was up seeing John at Peterhead yesterday, I have repeatedly asked for a visit and have always been refused, so in desperation I asked for the visit due to me in November, and it was granted.

Well, John has been on hunger strike since July. He resisted the forcible feeding for a good while, but submitted to the inevitable. Now he is being fed by a stomach tube twice daily. He has aged very much and has the look of a man who is going through torture. The Doctor all along has told me he is in good health, also the Prison Commissioners and I knew nothing about the forcible feeding until John told me in the presence of the doctor and two warders. Now, Ex-Inspector John Syme told me at the beginning of John's imprisonment that I need not worry about the fear of his going on hunger strike, as they dare not start forcible feeding without letting the relatives know.

Seemingly anything is law in regard to John. I hope you will make the atrocity public. We must get him out of their clutches. It is nothing else but slow murder. I feel very bitter at the way I have been treated. It was a terrible shock I received yesterday.

I see the premises have been raided and Lenin's pamphlet taken away, so you will be having enough worry.

I wish you good luck.

Yours fraternally,

A. MACLEAN.

The effect of this letter upon the whole labour movement was electric. A " John Maclean Defence Committee " was set up in London. Great demonstrations took place in Finsbury Park and in Stepney, London, in Glasgow, Clydebank, Leeds and other centres in the country.

William Gallacher, who was acting as deputy candidate for Maclean in the Gorbals constituency, appealed, as Maclean's deputy, to the Prison Commissioners for the opportunity to visit Maclean, but he was refused.

At the special Labour Party Conference held in November, Gallacher tried to raise the question and was ruled out by the platform on the ground that the Conference could only deal with the special questions of the General Election. On his insisting, however, so popular was the appeal that the platform had to yield, and a resolution was unanimously passed demanding the release of John Maclean.

Early in November, Sir Robert Munro, the Secretary for Scotland, was due to speak at a meeting in St. Andrew's Hall, Glasgow. In the House of Commons he had let slip a phrase in reply to a question about Maclean that subsequently proved embarrassing for him and the Government. Munro had said he was " not aware that this man was regarded by thousands as a hero and a martyr." The St. Andrew's Hall was packed waiting on him with the answer. Either Munro had thought better of it, or had been duly advised of what was in store for him. He decided not to attend. When the audience learned that Sir Robert was not coming a call was made in the body of the hall for the friends of Maclean to leave the meeting. The huge crowd trekked out leaving only a hundred or two behind.

Outside the hall a huge procession was formed up, and some 4,000 demonstrators marched through the streets to George Square singing revolutionary songs.

Almost immediately after this interrupted visit of Sir Robert Munro to Glasgow, and under the influence of the protests raised all over the country rumours began to circulate in Glasgow that Maclean was about to be released. On 3rd December the definite news came, Maclean was free !

His liberation was a great event for the whole labour movement. On arrival at Aberdeen from Peterhead, he was met and given a formal reception by friends of the I.L.P. who presented him with a travelling bag. Later in the day a social was held in the S.L.P. rooms in Aberdeen with Maclean as the guest of the company.

In Glasgow the excitement was intense. The train was expected to arrive at 4.30 p.m. from Aberdeen. Two hours before its arrival thousands of people gathered at George Square. A procession was formed and passed the time in singing revolutionary songs and shouting slogans.

When finally the train bearing John and Mrs. Maclean steamed into Buchanan Street Station, the reception was terrific. A horse drawn carriage was in readiness. The horse was taken out, and with the redoubtable warrior, Maclean, the ticket of leave man, seated in the box, the carriage was drawn by a group of sturdy workers.

Along the route of the procession enormous crowds gathered to salute Maclean who was standing up in the box-seat bearing a huge red banner, which had been presented to him immediately on his arrival. When the procession reached the corner of Jamaica Street and Argyle Street, one of the busiest thoroughfares in Glasgow, Maclean stopped the cavalcade for a moment. He called for three cheers for the Russian Revolution ; a second round of cheers for the German social revolution. Then he called for another three cheers, this time for the British social revolution. The journey was resumed across Jamaica Bridge to Carlton Place, where the District offices of the A.S.E. (now the A.E.U.) are situated. Short speeches were made, and Maclean was taken by taxi-cab to his home.

It happened that President Woodrow Wilson of the United States of America was on a visit to this country. Maclean immediately thought about the Socialists who were then in prison in America, and promptly wrote the following letter to Wilson :

Mr. Woodrow Wilson,
    President, U.S.A.
Sir,

You are here in Europe to negotiate a " democratic peace " as a Democrat. If so I wish you to prove your sincerity by releasing Tom Mooney, Eugene Debs, Bill Haywood, and all the others at present in prison as a consequence of their fight for " working class democracy " since the United States participated in the war. The working class Democracy of Britain forced the example to release me from Peterhead prison when I was undergoing a five years' sentence under D.O.R.A.

I therefore write you as an ease to my conscience, and a repayment to the " World working class Democracy " to release my above-mentioned friends and comrades.

The Clyde workers will send me as one of their delegates to the coming Peace Conference, and there, inside or outside the Conference Hall I shall challenge your U.S.A. delegates if my friends are not released. After that I shall tour America until you do justice to the real American champions of democracy.

Yours in deadly earnest,

JOHN MACLEAN.

Out of prison into the throes and excitement of a General Election was hardly the kind of rest Maclean needed. In other circumstances it would have been no real hardship. But John was a sick man, though he wouldn't admit it. Friends were hard put to it to keep him away from meetings. The crowd clamoured for him, naturally enough, but they did not know how ill he was. This they were to learn only at the eve of the poll meetings when Maclean made his appearance.

The adoption of John Maclean as the Labour Candidate for the Gorbals constituency was not surprising. The sitting member was George N. Barnes, a former Secretary of the A.S.E. and the official representative of the Labour Party. He won the seat in 1906, defeating Bonar Law the year the Tories were routed at the polls. The constituency was strong for Labour. But the fact that Barnes was pro-war and had done nothing to prevent arrests and deportations in the city, or to help to get the victims released after the events, had lost him much support in the constituency.

On the other hand feeling for John Maclean was strong because of his record as a socialist militant, and his being in prison raised issues of supreme importance for the whole labour movement. In this respect the selection of Maclean as the Labour candidate for Gorbals gave the fight a direct focus in the struggle for his release, and for the labour principles of liberty of thought and freedom of speech.

The selection of John Maclean as the Labour candidate for Gorbals was carried through the Divisional Labour Party according to rule. There was no hocus-pocus about it. He was the nominee of the local branch of the B.S.P., an affiliated body, and received the support, at a duly convened selection conference, of the great majority of the constituent bodies of the Divisional Party. His name was sent to the National Executive of the Labour Party for endorsement. The fact, however, that Barnes had not been repudiated by the National Executive put the latter in a dilemma, which was only solved when Barnes accepted the Coalition ticket and refused to follow the decisions of the Labour Party to take an independent course. Moreover, there was a group that preferred Barnes to Maclean. Thus the official endorsement of Maclean was withheld up to the last moment, and only grudgingly given when attempts to get the local bodies to reject Maclean had failed and there was no other alternative.

The meetings throughout the campaign were crowded and enthusiastic. On the unanimous invitation of the Divisional

Party William Gallacher, now M.P. for West Fife, was selected to be the Deputy standard bearer for Maclean, and right worthily did he fulfil his task. Gallacher worked like a trojan. For him Maclean in prison was the symbol of all that the Clyde workers stood for in those days. The fight for the release of Maclean was at once a token of working class solidarity and a challenge to the Government of Lloyd George. For the serious reasons of health to which we have referred Maclean was persuaded with much difficulty to keep off the platform, and he addressed no meetings until the eve of the Poll.

The fact that he would speak at the final rally was fully advertised, with amazing results. The whole suite of the St. Mungo Halls, the scenes of so many meetings for the release of Maclean, was fully booked, and on the final night the Reception, the Assembly, and the Grand Halls were crowded to over-capacity. Thousands failed to gain admission and it taxed all the available speakers to exhaustion to maintain a service indoors and out-doors. Never within living memory had there been witnessed such high enthusiasm.

Contrary to the wishes of his friends, who urged that he appear for a short time at the Grand Hall only, John insisted on speaking at all three meetings. The scenes of wild enthusiasm when he appeared passes description. His very presence was in itself a great victory for the campaign and a personal tribute to himself. And had he been in good health and able to hold the enthusiasm of these three meetings and the crowds outside, the story of his last days would have been very different.

As it was, he was unable to concentrate upon the problems of immediate importance in the election. Prison with hunger-striking and forcible feeding had obviously had graver effects than was generally known. Persecution obsessions and questions irrelevant to the Election made up the subject-matter of his speeches. The efforts of his friends to restrain him had not the slightest effect, except to provoke his feelings and to make matters worse. The wild enthusiasm with which he was received at each of his meetings evaporated in murmurs of sympathetic concern, many people leaving the meeting while he was speaking, obviously disturbed by the state of their friend and comrade's mind.

He polled 7,436 votes against 14,347 for Barnes. Who can say what might have happened in the Gorbals at that historic election, but for the eve of the poll meetings that revealed how terribly Maclean's health was impaired by his prison experience ?

A few days after the polling day it was arranged by friends to get him away for a holiday and rest. He was taken to the popular holiday resort, Rothesay. Here it was hoped he would find quietness and recuperate. But he did not know how to relax.

While in Rothesay he received the following communication from the Under-Secretary for Scotland :

Sir,

I am directed by the Secretary for Scotland to inform you that the King has been pleased to grant you a free pardon, in respect of your convictions at the High Court, Edinburgh, on 12th April, 1916, and 9th May, 1918, last, of offences against the Defence of the Realm Regulations. The Warrant granting the free pardon has been forwarded to the Court of Justiciary for record.

I am, Sir,

Your obedient Servant,

JAMES M. DODD.

Furious at the very suggestion of a " free pardon " he immediately wrote the following reply :

41 Victoria Street, Rothesay,
26th Dec., 1918

To Sir James M. Dodd,
Under Secy. for Scotland.

Sir,—Would you be so kind as to inform the Secretary for Scotland that I do not accept your assertion that " the King has granted me a free pardon."

Not " the King " (who should be in Holland with his cousin), but the fighting workers of Britain, have regained me my freedom and a healthy fear of those workers has induced you and your friends to try this bluff of a " free pardon." All the time, however, you are trying to pester my wife and myself through your detestable spies, popularly called detectives. I welcome their attentions, as it is a sign that you are foaming at the mouth at having to release me.

My immediate reply to this is a demand from the Government, through the Scottish Office, for the hundred and fifty pounds (£150) the cost of recovery after my release last time and this, from your cold-blooded treatment in those infernos Peterhead and Perth.

I made a claim last time for seventy-six pounds (£76) and was refused. The new demand includes that sum, and this new demand I intend to insist upon until it is met by the next government or until the workers assume full control of the British Empire.

Yours sincerely,

JOHN MACLEAN.

It will be seen from this letter that Maclean not only refused to acknowledge any justification for his arrests and imprisonment, but took the offensive against the Government with a claim for personal injury, as a result of the treatment he received in prison. Needless to say no such compensation was forthcoming.

CHAPTER 13

KEEPING CAPITALISM BUSY AT HOME

CONSIDERING the treatment Maclean received in prison, it would not have been surprising had he come out a completely broken man. That this term of imprisonment took an enormous toll from his nervous system, there is no gainsaying. He was irritable, highly strung, and extremely suspicious of those around him, even his closest and most loyal friends. He was certain, and with every justification, that the authorities were bent on destroying him physically. But he was not to be broken so easily. In spite of everything his tremendous reserves of vitality, carried him through a period of extraordinary and astonishing activity in 1919.

G

He began with a special New Year message to readers of " The Call."

  " Greetings to all comrades and the mass of the working class who forced the Cabinet to release me. George Barnes' claim that he got my release is a lie as base as his betrayal of our class. He and the cabinet members were really afraid of their lives, and rightly so ; for the workers have now reached a stage in the evolution of our class when they will punish their enemies in the great class war."

Taking advantage of the presence of President Wilson in Great Britain, " The Scottish Home Rule Association " had prepared a memorandum and presented it to President Wilson claiming separate representation for Scotland at the coming Peace Congress. This " Memorial " had been sent to a number of organisations, to Scottish M.P.s and parliamentary candidates soliciting their support. Among those endorsing the " memorial " was the Scottish T.U.C.

On being invited by R. Erskine of Mar to sign it, Maclean replied : That he was " in favour of a Parliament or Soviet of workers for Scotland with headquarters in Scotland." But such, he contended, would not come through negotiations of Scotsmen with the quack Peace Conference, but rather through the revolutionary efforts of the Scottish working class itself. He went on to refer to the futility of expecting President Wilson to do anything for Scotland, since " he is the representative of brutally blatant capitalism in America." " Were I to thank anyone for actual services rendered to the cause of Home Rule, I would certainly thank my glorious comrades, Lenin, etc. The only thanks they would appreciate would be the successful revolutionising of Scotland by its wage-slave class.

  " My life has been spent in making for this goal, and this year I mean to do more than ever for the ending of capitalism in Scotland—as elsewhere in the world—and the establishment of the socialist republic in which alone we can have Home Rule."

He finishes by recommending the laird to read Marx's " Capital " and his other writings, as well as Engels' " Socialism, Utopian and Scientific."

This letter is interesting for the appreciation it gives of

President Wilson and the Peace Conference which was about to open ; of Maclean's views on Home Rule (which will be developed later), but particularly in showing his fixed determination to assist in bringing about the revolution in Scotland.

In the third week in January an article appears in " The Call " under the title, " Now's the Day, and Now's the Hour," in which he develops his ideas. He refers to the class war now going on upon an international scale and asks the questions : " How must we act ? " There is much talk, he says, about a General Strike to enforce a withdrawal of the interventionist forces from Russia and Germany. " That to some of us on the Clyde is too idealistic." Were the masses revolutionary socialists, he replies, it would be all right, but they are not our way of thinking. We should have no success, he declares, as " the Government has the majority of the Trade Union leaders in the hollow of its hand, and can easily manipulate them against us." (Prophetic anticipation indeed !) " Some of us on the Clyde have another line, and that is to save Russia by developing the revolution in Britain no later than this yea.."

And the justification for such a hope ? Maclean sees this in a number of possible conditions. He sees a big struggle to dispose of the trebled production ; a glut of goods which, he says, in five years time will force America and Britain into war for fear of revolution through unemployment and hunger. Already, he noted, demobilisation was creating problems of unemployment. The only solution was a drastic reduction in the hours of labour per week, and this, he insists, " is the economic issue to unify the workers in the war against capitalism."

In the meantime a number of industrial clouds were hanging over the country, much unrest and threats of strike action. Maclean attached great importance to the role of the miners in this period. He had placed his services at the disposal of the Miner's Reform movement. A first campaign had begun amongst the Lothian miners with a week's mission to start unofficial committees, and, declared Maclean, if the Miners' Federation of Great Britain does not make up its mind at Southport on 14th February to enforce its programme, they (i.e. the unofficial movement) would call a strike around the middle of February.

He made an appeal for the formation of committees and for preparation, and concluded :

" With a determined revolutionary minority we shall be able to take control of the country and the means of production at once, and hold them tight, through disciplined production under the workshop committees, and the district and national councils."

" Through the Co-operative movement we shall be able to control the full distribution of the necessities of life, and so win the masses over to socialism."

" All revolutions have started on seemingly trifling economic and political issues. Ours is to direct the workers to the goal by pushing forward the Miners' programme, and backing up our ' black brigade.' "

The miners, however, were not to play the leading role. The Shorter Hours' movement had gripped the engineering and shipbuilding workers on the Clyde and was already well advanced towards strike action. The Forty Hours Strike, which broke out within a few days of the appearance of Maclean's article, embraced the vast majority of the workers in Scotland. In included the miners, it is true, but the decisive role was in the hands of the engineering workers, and they were far from thinking of revolution. It was a disappointment to Maclean, which he retained to the end, that the engineering trades did not stay their hand till March, when he believed the whole of the miners could have been got to strike together with the engineers.

In an article on the " Forty Hours' Strike*" which he wrote a week later he says, " Some of us would have preferred the miners to lead off, but historical events never start and shape themselves as we plan them." Undaunted he appeals for mutual confidence and self-reliance, and concludes, " Into the fight and make it a really revolutionary one."

In a pamphlet written immediately following the collapse of the Forty Hours' Strike, entitled, " Sack Dalrymple : Sack Stevenson," Maclean gives his appraisal of the events attending the George Square affair on " Bloody Friday," 31st January,

* For details of the 40 Hours Strike see W. Gallacher, M.P., " Revolt on the Clyde " and " Pioneering Days," by T. Bell.

1919. He refers to the spread of the Forty Hours Movement in Scotland, the Forty-Four Hours Movement in Belfast ; the strike on the Tyneside on the meal-time question, and says, " In the temper of the people at this time the Government feared a revolution such as had swept Germany. . . . The movement had to be nipped in the bud, and the opportunity presented itself in the move of the workers who appealed to the Lord Provost of Glasgow to force the employers to grant the shorter working week."

The Lord Provost, who had been approached on the Wednesday told the strikers to come back on Friday. Meanwhile the trap was being prepared, the tramway service providing the means for provocation. The strikers had calculated on a tramway stoppage to paralyse the transport within the city. There was every reason to expect it to come off, large numbers did respond. But Dalrymple, the General Manager of the tramways, got busy, and by means of intimidation succeeded in getting a few to stay at work and a skeleton service was run. Dalrymple planned that trams should run through George Square, although the Square was packed with an immense crowd. The authorities evidently calculated on angry feelings between the strikers and the " blacklegs " leading to incidents, calculations which proved to be exact.

Maclean fastens the blame for the " riot " on Dalrymple and upon Chief Constable Stevenson. Had no cars ran through the Square, declares Maclean, there would have been no cause for " riot." This is only partially true, for it ignores the " feint " of the mounted policeman, who tumbled his horse near the entrance to the Municipal Chambers and led to an open conflict between the police and the crowd.

It is certain that Dalrymple had for a long time been ruling the tramwaymen with a heavy hand. He had fought against the tramwaymen belonging to a trade union. A strike for this right was broken in 1911. He kept the workers in an atmosphere of suspicion unfavourable to organisation. The tramwaymen's private affairs were pried into and those who showed any socialist or trade union sympathies were summarily dismissed. Men entering a public house with any part of their uniform on were summoned before his under-strappers to explain their conduct.

In this pamphlet Maclean cites evidence of the species of intimidation to which the workers were subjected, and apportions a certain blame upon Bailie A. Turner, who was the organiser of the Municipal Employees' Association, for failing to stand up to Dalrymple. He cites cases of tramway workers who were hounded out of the service, and tracked across the North of England and black-listed everywhere by Dalrymple. " Had Turner even played the man inside the council he could have hammered Dalrymple until the victims were allowed back to work or Dalrymple himself cleared out of the service." And Maclean exonerates the tramwaymen from exclusive blame for working.

Maclean also directed his attack upon Chief Constable Stevenson for his complicity with Dalrymple in causing the " riot." He cites evidence of the Chief Constable's irritating methods of using traffic regulations to disturb the socialist meetings in the centre of the city usually held on Sunday nights. In Glasgow Green no one was allowed to sell literature at the meetings without the permission of the Chief Constable. Maclean himself had been " booked " several times. " While it is evident," writes Maclean, " that Dalrymple is primarily to blame (for the riot) yet Stevenson comes in a close second."

As for the remedy, Maclean insists it is necessary to sack both of them. And he urges, " A solid vote for the labour candidates is the first step. Labour should control the police and prevent their mobilisation against the workers. With satirical irony he suggests that " the first step should be the transfer of Stevenson to some such ' safe ' place as Dublin or Cork."

Some socialists, says Maclean, may object to voting Labour. In the circumstances they have to choose between the Labour men now standing and the capitalist defenders of " property " and high rents. The Labour candidates may not be all some of us would like, but it is better to send them to power and so test them in the light of experience. An interesting anticipation of Lenin's advice in " Left-Wing Communism." And he finishes with " a final appeal for a resounding blow in Labour's counter-offensive. Away with Dalrymple : Away with Stevenson : Into power with Labour."

With the temporary quietude in Scotland following the collapse of the Forty Hours Strike, Maclean crosses the border and embarks on a hurricane propaganda tour. At Workington and Whitehaven in Cumberland he has large meetings, but great interruptions from the local Discharged Soldiers' and Sailors' organisations. At Barrow-in-Furness the Town Hall is packed to overflowing before the time to start. He speaks for one hour and three-quarters, and then addresses an overflow meeting for fifty minutes.

He attends the 8th Annual Conference of the B.S.P. in Sheffield in April, moves an emergency resolution on Russia, Hungary and Bavaria in defence of the revolution in those countries and calling for hands off from the interventionists. He moves a resolution on Conscription which " welcomes the declaration of the Miners' Federation that in conjunction with organised labour it will take steps, both political and industrial, calculated to render abortive all attempts to continue conscription and urges the workers of Great Britain to present a united and determined resistance to the Government's effort to give new life to militarism in the interest of the possessing classes."

In moving this resolution, he said that the conscript army is being maintained in order to crush the revolutionary movements on the continent. We must deprive the governing class of their army. *The capitalist class must be kept busy at home.* That sentence, " the capitalist class must be kept busy at home," epitomises the whole activity of Maclean throughout the war and post-war period.

The B.S.P. Conference over, he goes further afield to South Wales. Here again he has to face the opposition of the local branch of the Discharged Soldiers' and Sailors' Society and an attempt to wreck his meeting. So successful, however, was Maclean that when the hall had to be vacated for a Cinema show as advertised, the crowd eagerly adjourned to the mountain side to carry on the meeting.

From South Wales he goes to Bradford. A great assembly cheers him to the echo. He predicts the coming of another war, and urges that only the action of the workers can prevent it. He makes a special appeal for the Clyde Defence Fund, and raises £9.

It is May Day in Glasgow. 150,000 people march through the streets to Glasgow Green. Maclean is the prominent speaker, with Countess Markiewicz, the Irish rebel. In the evening he is speaking at Paisley. On the 25th May he is again the chief speaker on Glasgow Green demanding the release of " Eugene V. Debs and all other comrades throughout the world who are in prison."

The following week he is in Colne Valley, where he addressed five meetings. He speaks under the auspices of the Trades Council at Huddersfield. A resolution is presented to this meeting :

" Condemning the Government for its failure to carry out its schemes of reconstruction, for keeping in prison the conscientious objectors, the Clyde strike leaders, and other champions of labour ; for continuing conscription ; for intervention in Russia, Hungary ; for its brutal peace terms imposed on the German workers, and for its army secret document."

The resolution then proposes a Conference of all unions with the object of carrying out a general strike on these issues. " If the Trade Unions fail, then we should support an unofficial general strike at this critical juncture in the history of the world and the world's workers."

Back again in Glasgow he is the chief speaker at huge demonstration in Glasgow Green, demanding the release of Gallacher and the other prisoners following the Forty Hours Strike.

A few weeks later on, Maclean is the chief speaker at a reception given to Gallacher on his release by the Paisley Trades and Labour Council.

Thus between May Day and August Maclean had addressed meetings in Colne Valley, Durham, Ayrshire, Edinburgh, West Lothians, Lanarkshire, Glasgow, and Fifeshire. In the latter county he held nine meetings inside two weeks. " Keeping capitalism busy at home ! "

CHAPTER 14

CO-OPERATION AND PRICES

IN September 1919 the Trades Union Congress met at Glasgow. Maclean followed the proceedings with the highest interest. For him the central issue of the Congress was the question of direct action for political purposes. The war of intervention in Russia was going on and at home a big campaign was being pushed for increased production.

Writing in " The Call," Maclean draws attention to the attitude of the Parliamentary Committee of the T.U.C. By a majority of two the Parliamentary Committee had refused to agree to recommend to the T.U.C. the proposal for a Special Congress to discuss how to put a stop to the war of intervention in Soviet Russia, the continuation of military conscription and other political issues. The miners led by Bob Smillie insisted, and the Parliamentary Committee was defeated. Maclean attacked the Parliamentary Committee of the T.U.C. for what he called " manipulating the miners off the P.C." Without the miners, says Maclean, the P.C. can only be a sickly shadow. He urges every union to go to the Special Congress pledged to a general strike if a general election has not been publicly and authoritatively summoned (the appointment of a Special Committee by open card vote and not to leave things to the Parliamentary Committee). He wants to see this special committee and the P.C. replaced by a permanently sitting Labour Committee or Council. His third point was a drive for action through the workshop movement.

In the meantime the Government made the next move, by an attack upon the Railwaymen. The Government had granted the Locomotive and Firemen of the A.S.L.E. and F. a standard wage, but refused similar terms to the N.U.R. The latter had to take strike action. For Maclean this was the Government's reply to the miners' success at the T.U.C. The Government calculated, says Maclean, upon the uncertainty of J. H. Thomas, the N.U.R. leader ; on the desertion of Bromley, leader of the Locomotive and Firemen, on the use of the

Middle Class Union, and upon the mobilisation of transport, oil, coal and the Press. The Government hopes, thinks Maclean, that with these powers enhanced, the Special Congress might be relied upon to vote against " direct action " to save Russia, and to save the workers from conscription and military intervention in strikes.

Can the miners afford to wait a month or two, until March 1920, if need be ? " I believe they can," replies Maclean, " if they apply the Ca' canny policy and are backed by other workers. Let us perfect the organisation," he says, " and see that a Central Committee of Labour is established.

" This attack on the railwaymen will consolidate the workers as a class, and show the capitalist nature of the Government more than anything else. The unity of the railway workers is surprisingly encouraging, and rallying the working-class generally.

" A General Strike should be avoided for the moment as the Government has shown its preparedness, amongst other things, by its control of food and vehicles.

" A General Strike must have the impetus of a labour attack. The impetus is now on the Government side.

" A respite will enable the workers' drift towards Labour to increase, will enable us to clarify the vision of our class and perfect industrial organisation on a sound class basis, and will give us the time to show the Co-operative movement that the Middle Class Union, largely composed of private traders, and their kith and kin in the professional services, has as its end the general onslaught on labour, the crushing of co-operation—the Commissariat department of Labour's Army."

Maclean here shows a surprising degree of cautiousness and judgment for one usually impetuous in his zeal for the political strike. His reference to the setting up of a permanent labour council is a striking anticipation of the future General Council of the Trades Union Congress, that was to emerge two years later, though even still incomplete. His treatment of the part to be played by Co-operative Movement, which he next takes up is equally arresting.

Ever since the sending of the foodship to Dublin in 1911 to help the Transport Workers, the Co-operative movement had come to be looked upon by the workers in general as Labour's

Commissariat Department. The T.U.C. were making over-
tures at this time to the Co-operative movement in anticipation
of big labour struggles ahead. A statement made by Fred
Bramley, then secretary of the T.U.C., provoked the " London
Letter " writer of " The Scotsman " in the issue for 18th
October, 1919, to say : " It is doubtful whether the advanced
wing of the Labour movement will be at all grateful to Mr.
Fred Bramley for his disclosure that in future strikes affecting
the community as a whole it is being arranged to introduce the
machinery of the Co-operative Societies for the support of the
striking Trade Unionists threatened with a shortage of supplies. The idea is to ensure the distribution of food supplies
and the payment of benefit by issuing through the various
branches of the Co-operative movement food coupons or loans
from the Co-operative Wholesale's Bank on the security of
Trade Union assets."

Maclean replies to the " London Letter " in an article in
" The Call," and says : " we cannot but be pleased at Bramley's disclosure, because it will hearten us to push the scheme
everywhere, especially after the scabbery of the Middle Class
Union, which is mainly composed of the shop keeping class or
the high paid flunkies of the capitalist multiple distributive
companies. The fight of the future centres around food and
the armed forces. If by publicity we can win the armed forces
and thus get access to the food, the Co-operative movement can
help us to ensure that our class is regularly and properly fed
during the crisis."

The Scottish Workers' Committees were that week (25th
October) holding a Conference " to discuss the construction of
industrial and social committees in each area,"* and to project
plans fitted to enable food to circulate freely for the benefit of
the workers (and the Social Committee will see that the food is
rationally distributed when the crisis comes). Maclean trusts
that the rank and file everywhere will follow suit or go one
better.

* The idea of forming Social Committees, after the manner of the
Soviets of Russia was at this time freely canvassed by the Scottish
workers' committees, an offshoot of the defunct Clyde Workers' Committee.

" I am of the opinion," he says, " that in London and other areas where Co-operation is still weak, the movement could be quickly rushed into a postiion of supremacy if organised Labour used its funds and its machinery to establish and strengthen the movement." He appeals to Bramley and others in responsible positions to take up the matter at once, and ends : " Permit me also to suggest that the three great Labour organisations ought now to set out jointly to map Britain into areas, and send the best speakers everywhere to organise demonstrations and work gate meetings, to see that every worker is in a Union affiliated to the Labour Party, and that every worker is also in the co-operative movement. . . . Let Labour earnestly now spend its hundreds of thousands on a thunderous publicity campaign. Spread and knit up must be the policy, for now the day of victory is at hand."

Inspired by the march of events Maclean urges the British Socialist Party to advance a united programme, to include :

Full socialisation of the mines and other trustified industries.
Full industrial control by the workers involved, modified to permit use of the Co-operative movement.
Control of education of the Workers.
A 30 hours' working week.
Fifty per cent. increase in wages.
Communally produced houses.
Withdrawal of British troops from all parts of the world.
Abolition of the Army and Navy and establishment of a Workers' Defence Force.
Transfer of the functions of Parliament to the Labour Central Committee.

" Was I wrong," he exclaims, " when I urged as Labour's prayer, We shall this year kill capitalism ? "

Reasoning from the events of the year Maclean never wavered in his hopes for a social revolution. Speaking at a large demonstration in the Kingsway Hall, London, on the occasion of the 2nd Anniversary of the Russian Revolution he declared : " We in this country are moving in the rapids of revolution. The Shop Stewards' Committees are driving forward the ' labour leaders,' especially in the mining districts. The Spartacists of Germany are preparing a revolution and soon our chance will come.

" The Triple Alliance of Labour must come to take the place of Parliament. On with the class war. Let our cry be not ' Nationalisation,' but ' Socialisation.' The doom of capitalism is at hand."

In the month of November Maclean took up the question of prices which were then soaring high to the disadvantage of the working class. He began a series of articles (and wrote, in all, seven) with the startling headline : " The Cure for High Prices : Burn Bradbury."*

He starts off with a reference to the fact that :

The Government had announced in November 1919 a reduction of 10/- on the ton of coal. " A paralytic fit, or funk, which is it ? " asks Maclean. But whatever the case, " I trust," he writes, " the Government has again miscalculated if it imagines that a 10/- drop in the ton price of coal will buy off the miners' attempt to get a united Labour attack on the shameful cost of living." Supposing the average family burns two cwts. of coal a week, the saving is only 1/——a mere trifle these days." He suspects the epileptic fears of the Government proves its criminal guilt in robbing the miner or the consumer, or both.

He then takes the Board of Trade's index number for the retail price of twenty-three articles of food. " We find," he writes, " that the number for the year 1896 was about 92, and for July 1911 about 117. The November issue of the Labour Gazette tells us that food prices in large cities were 136 per cent. higher than in July 1914, in small towns and villages 127 per cent. ; or an average for the United Kingdom of 131 per cent. The 136 drops to about 130 per cent., if we take in other outlays, such as the dwelling, clothes and household utensils. So says the Board of Trade. Were inferior quality taken into consideration the average increase would far exceed 130 per cent.

" As, however, we are but meantime tracing the index number for food prices about the number in October 1919 for larger towns, it works out at about 276, and the general average at about 269.

" The ratio of 92 to 276 is the same as £1 to £3, so that on

* John Bradbury's name figures on the new one-pound and ten-shilling notes issued during the war.

food alone we have to spend to-day £3 for every pound in 1896. In 1904 the Board of Trade examined the food Budget of 1900 families and found the average outlay to be 22/6 per week. That was the same as 20/2 in 1896. These families ought now to be spending at least £3 to get the same quantity of food (the quality camouflaged of course).

" The percentage spent in food out of the weekly outlay was about 67 per cent., in 1904. If we make it 75 per cent. to-day, then the family outlay would require to be at least £4 per week. This squares with the estimate made by Rowntree in his book, ' The Human Needs of Labour,' issued in 1916."

As to the immediate cause of the high prices he examines the Report of the Committee on Currency and Foreign Exchange, and finds that in June 1914 the legal tender money in circulation or in the banks amounted to nearly £180 millions, of which £123 millions were gold coins, and on 10th July, 1918 the total was £383 millions, of which only £40 millions consisted of gold. In the latter year £28 millions of Bradbury's were covered by gold, and £230 millions uncovered.

" To lower prices," says Maclean, " the obvious course is to withdraw the Bradbury's from circulation, and return to a gold money system." " Therefore," he suggests, " the slogan of Labour should be ' Burn Bradbury,' that is to say, the Bradbury Treasury One Pound and Ten Shilling Notes. Let that be the cry at the Special Trade Union Congress ; let that be the cry at your trade union branch meeting ; let that be the cry at all public meetings . . . ' Burn Bradbury ! ' "

While not opposing the demands for higher wages, Maclean insisted upon lower prices as the better remedy for the high cost of living, since lower prices would benefit the unorganised workers who were hardest hit by the high cost of living. That is why he made lower prices a cardinal point in the programme he issued in the course of the next few months, in May 1920.

All the arguments brought forward by Maclean about the causes of the rising cost of living and high prices were just. He was also correct in showing that the enormous flood of paper money was a potent means leading to high prices, and that the withdrawal of this paper money, other things being equal, would bring prices down to their proper level.

The flood of paper money referred to by Maclean was largely due to the war, when, as always, the expenses of a Government exceed the revenue from normal resources. The consequent rise in prices due to the depreciated paper money undoubtedly strikes the working class hardest. They suffer most because wages always tend to lag behind prices. It was all the more important to explain fully the reasons for the emission of paper money. It was necessary to bring out clearly the responsibility and the means at the disposal of the Government to remedy the evil, and to put forward some positive and practical proposals that would bring conviction to the working class.

Since the problem of paper money was connected with the Government's need of the wherewithal to meet its heavy additional expenditure, the demand for a mechanical cancellation of the superfluous paper money, unaccompanied by any other measures, was an unrealistic one. In order to return from an inflated to a normal currency it was necessary to reduce the great discrepancy between State revenue and State expenditure. This could have been done in two ways : on the one hand by a repudiation of that large part of the National Debt which was held by big financial capitalists ; on the other by the creation of more solid state resources—for example, by a Capital Levy on the wealthy property owners, and/or by the nationalisation of essential industries and their development as a State enterprise—a measure which could have greatly strengthened State resources without any sacrifice of the wages and conditions of the workers employed, but on the contrary with an improvement in them.

Then the call for the Government to withdraw the excessive paper money could have been turned into a real political demand and found widespread support. As it was, the slogan, " Burn Bradbury," found no response among serious and practical minded trade unionists. This appears to have been a case in which Maclean's usually clear and sound judgment on economic questions was clouded by the impetuous zeal of an ardent agitator.

CHAPTER 15

IS CAPITALISM COLLAPSING ?

MACLEAN's amazing activity in 1919 was not confined to propaganda meetings, and the writing of articles on the question
of prices and paper currency, and articles on the Trade Union
Congress and the role of the miners. Side by side with these he
wrote articles of theoretical importance, attacking certain
views that were beginning to spread then about the collapse of
capitalism. In an article which he wrote for " The Call " in
August 1919, he takes to task those who seemed to be carried
away with the publication of the book by the American writer,
Kahn, entitled " The Collapse of Capitalism," and by alarmist
articles and speeches about the vast accumulation of credit,
paper money and bills.

Capitalism, he contends, is not based on Credit or paper
money, but on the production of commodities for surplus value
in the form of interest, profits and rent. The conditions are
sources of raw materials, machinery and organisation, skilled
labour and markets. He draws attention to the vast extension
of plant (fixed capital) with the war, and to the resources of
labour power which have been swollen by a mighty new army
of women workers. The conditions of production being
doubled in comparison with pre-war times, the possibilities of
surplus value are treble that of 1914. If, he continues, more
gold is needed to back up the paper media of commodity
circulation, that, he thinks, can easily and plentifully be
obtained from industrial sources and the gold mines ; or silver
can be used as unlimited legal tender, as in Britain in the
eighteenth century. And, he emphasises, the settled policy of
the London bankers and Government is to induce the workers
to toil harder than ever. Compulsion through scientific
management, inducement through bonus, profit sharing and
similar payments by results methods are merely supplements
to the alarmist appeals to save the Empire by reducing the
time and cost of production.

(Here he cannot resist a dig at the anti-Marxists. Everyone, he says, now adheres to the labour-time theory of value except J. Ramsay Macdonald, some capitalist economists and the mass of the trade union leaders and labour men.)

He sees in every economic preparation of Britain—improved machinery, industrial research, trustification, standardisation, scientific management, applied industrial psychology and physiology, bank amalgamation and its world extension, state unification of mines, railways, electricity production and supply, slightly reduced hours, capitalist industrial unionism, the Overseas Department, etc.—a vital preparation for the coming trade war with America. Indeed, he remarks, never were the capitalists more lively, more aggressive.

And what were the expectations of the socialists ? he asks. " Our hopes lay first in the Miners' Federation leading the workers to battle on an immediate programme that would have ultimately involved capital and labour in a revolutionary conflict. But, by the introduction of the Coal Commission and the Industrial Peace Conference with its committee, Lloyd George prevented a general strike until Britain won the stakes at Paris."

Lloyd George's pronouncement against nationalisation of the mines and in favour of trustification, the Minimum Rate of Wages Commission Bill and the Hours of Employment (No. 2) Bill, his denunciation of the miners for reducing output—all those, says Maclean, have " converted the miners' attack into a defence with a host of official and unofficial traitors in the ranks of the miners weakening even the defence."

" That is no evidence of collapse, is it ? " he asks.

Our hopes, he goes on, were then transferred to the Triple Alliance. A ballot for a strike was determined upon when Churchill made a speech assuring the " Labour Leaders " Britain was withdrawing her troops from Russia. They met and thanked him for the excuse it afforded them for suspending the ballot. Meantime the press is working up the opinion behind Henderson and Clynes that " Direct Action " is out of fashion and we should wait for a possible general election at the end of the year. The Government has plenty of agents in the ranks of labour to spread this rumour. And, he adds, " the capitalist class that can manoeuvre ' Labour ' backwards and forwards in this way shows no signs of having lost its kick ! "

After referring to the role Britain was playing in international affairs, the presence of the Highland Division camped near Mansfield, Notts, ready for the miners, and to Ireland, " being incited to revolt so that John the Bully may give her a long sleep," he says, " Such do not appear to be the signs of collapse."

In the month of November 1919, he returns again to the question : " Is capitalism collapsing ? " In a rejoinder to the American writer on economic questions, Mary E. Marcy, he said, " At the beginning of the year Kahn's ' Collapse of Capitalism' had great vogue at economics classes and greatly influenced class leaders and teachers. At the time I said Kahn's book was bad economics and bad Marxism. If capitalism is going to collapse from purely financial causes then there is no need for effort, no need for prosecuting the class war."

At Easter time he goes on, " The British Press raised the alarm about financial collapse to justify the withholding of supplies of credit to France, because France was making extravagant demands at the Peace Conference." In other words, " Britain used this collapse bleat to justify a financial blockade of France. France yielded all right. However, certain of the best Marxists in the South Wales coalfields were deceived by the press stunt, all the more readily as they had been swept away by Kahn's book that supplemented their contention that the gradually increasing pressure on the profits of the capitalists would in the end reduce these to the vanishing point with the inevitable collapse of the present system. When I showed the leading articles dealing with France's obstinacy our comrades at once realised the game."

Maclean observes that the British governing class are very apprehensive of America's menace to Britain's grip on the world markets, and are following the tactics of America. Trustification is proceeding rapidly. American machinery and scientific methods of speed up are universally being adopted to increase output to the American level. The miners and other workers have been denounced for " Ca' canny " and told that if production is not increased Britain will lose markets to America, and will be ruined. To prevent bankruptcy production must be increased. " I assure my audience," he goes on to say, "that if British capitalism is going to collapse through restricted production, there ought to be ca' canny in real earnest."

He is convinced that Austin Chamberlain and Lloyd George have raised the financial alarm in the House of Commons with a view to influencing America to hurry over her signature to the Peace Treaty and to take over some of Britain's bad debts amongst the Allies, as well as to prevent British workers demanding more money and to prepare them for a future break in wages.

Quoting Lord Milner's speech in the Lords when he said that prices could not be reduced drastically, as wages would have to be brought down as well, and that would involve a revolution, Maclean retorts : "That is it precisely . . . not financial collapse, but the attempt to escape from a financially tight corner must involve working class resistance, leading right on to the revolution."

Recapitulating his view on the increased output of gold since 1890, the increase in paper money and the effect on prices, he concluded : "With the trustification of banks and insurance companies and their closer and closer grip over the British Cabinet we may depend upon it that expediency will be resorted to to prevent financial collapse as at the beginning of the war. Paper notes will continue in vogue, and the exchange of goods in the world will become more and more by barter, as before the war, with the need for sending only small quantities of gold hither and thither. View it as I may I cannot see the possibility of a financial collapse automatically arising out of the contradictions of the capitalist process of production. The great contradiction is the opposition of classes leading to the collapse of the system through the mighty, resounding blows of a world united labour."

And the lesson ? "We must agitate, educate, and organise more boldly and vigorously than before. Let us remember that although the trade union and political leaders of the working class have been afraid to be as audacious as the leaders of capitalism, have failed as ever at the critical moment, and will do it again, nevertheless the mass of the people are coming more and more towards our position.

"Therein lies salvation. The safety of society rests not in

the hands of a few (leaders or heroes), but in those of the masses
of mankind, conscious or unconscious—drifting our way. The
greater the drift the more the props of capitalism will vanish,
and hence the pending collapse of capitalism. . . . On with the
fight ; On with the class war.''

CHAPTER 16

A PROGRAMME OF ACTION

In 1920 Maclean resurrected '' The Vanguard,'' which had been
seized in 1916 following the historic St. Andrew's Hall meeting
with Lloyd George. It appeared in time for the May Day
Demonstration. The paper is described as '' a monthly
socialist organ,'' and all articles, letters and business communications are to be addressed to J. Maclean, 42 Auldhouse
Road, Newlands, Glasgow, his private residence.

The first of two short editorials is of interest for the light it
throws upon Maclean's outlook then on the working class
movement. He speaks of '' the skill and cuteness of the
Government in preventing a strike of the miners, who might
have received the support of the rest of the workers to the
detriment of the British proposals at the Peace Conference, to
the defeat of Britain's anti-Russian policy, and to the en-
dangerment of British capitalism itself.''

The scope given to Smillie and his colleagues at the Coal
Commission he regards '' as a farce to stave off revolt.'' The
Government then set about the breaking up of the miner's
reform movement and succeeded in driving Smillie out of the
fighting ranks, defeating direct action for nationalisation of the
mines and isolating the miners from the other trade unions.

At the same time, he goes on, it has paralysed the B.S.P. and
the S.L.P. and may do the same with the I.L.P. as well, so as
to clear the ground for a safe and sane Labourism, safe and
sane because '' dominated by ideas of the reform of capitalism
rather than a determination to destroy capitalism and in-
augurate the Workers' Republic.'' And, he explains, '' dissatisfaction with the plight of the B.S.P., maimed by this year's

onslaught of capitalism has compelled us to resurrect ' the Vanguard,' in the hope of concentrating the minds of the workers on the revolution to be gone through in this country, as on the one gone through already in Russia."

How to bring about this revolution dominates the whole of Maclean's thought and action in this period. He had the sound instinct that before the revolution was possible there must be above all unity of aims and purpose in the ranks of the working class. This was far from being the case then, even among the socialists and militants. To achieve this unity and solidarity in action Maclean was obsessed with the idea of a Programme of demands. He formulated such a programme and for the next few months kept it to the front in all his propaganda. It is published in this first number of the resurrected " Vanguard " with the caption, running across the front page, " A Fighting Programme Needed."

In a preamble to the suggested programme Maclean explains the reasons why he thinks the time is opportune to launch such a programme. He starts off by examining the arguments of two types of socialists in the socialist movement.

" In the ranks of the socialist movement," he says, " are still to be found those who parrot to-day, as they argued in 1914, that no social revolution is possible until the vast majority of the wage-earners are conscious revolutionary socialists. They remind us of the socialists at the other extreme who argued that society would slowly evolve into socialism with an accompanying improvement in the lot of the labouring class and an increase in their happiness ! "

The reference to the latter type is a thrust at the Fabian-Labour leaders of those days. He reminds them that real wages had been falling since 1900, and that after trying political action through the Labour Party the more intelligent workers urged the others to direct action.

" The former type appear likewise to be blind to the responsibility, nay probability, of a revolutionary impulse of the masses as a consequence of an economic breakdown on the continent leading to a similar phenomenon here. Should that impulse come and the masses get on the move, this human avalanche will sweep the political power of the present ruling class into the historic past and assume power itself. . . . Willy-nilly the workers must move forward in the establishment of socialism, whether fully conscious or not."

In support of his thesis he takes Russia as " the great class instance." Economic breakdown preceded political breakdown. The Liberal-capitalists led by Miliukoff came to power, to be succeeded by Kerensky ; unable to retain the confidence of the people in their despair, he too was cast aside and the Bolsheviks were thrust into power, " not on account of the people's sudden adhesion to Marxism, but largely due to the immediate programme proclaimed by the Bolsheviks—Peace, Bread, Land."

Looking back after the 25 years experience and the fuller knowledge of the history of the revolution in Russia and the role of the Bolshevik Party it is easy enough to detect a certain measure of error, of belief in " spontaneity " and " mechanical revolution." in Maclean's ideas on this question. The order of events as they unrolled themselves then in Russia are correctly placed. But the conscious role of the Bolshevik Party, the political leadership, its planned preparation for the October uprising, is missing.

Maclean seized on a material factor of the highest importance: the need for concrete slogans that correspond to the needs of the masses. He would do the same here in this country. He sees production slackening down and people starving. Prices are going up. There is unrest and grumbling. He recalls the defeat, at the Trade Union Congress in March of that year, of the proposal for direct action to nationalise the mines, and the joy of the capitalist press thereat, and says, " we may safely conclude that nothing is more dreaded in autocratic circles than the general strike."

" Very well then," he goes on, " ours is the duty to formulate an immediate programme that will appeal to all workers, and so prepare them for united action. We must have such a programme *that no capitalist government can concede* (Italics ours), one that necessarily must bring about a clash of the dominant class ; a programme that may not immediately inspire the workers to action, but one that in a crisis might so rouse them that by effective *spontaneous* effort they will sweep the capitalists out of power."

There seems a considerable confusion in ideas here. An immediate programme that would appeal to all workers must surely, if it did appeal to them, rouse them to action. If it did not immediately inspire them to action it could only be because the programme had no connection with realities. On the other hand, if the programme was to be one, and proclaimed as such, that no capitalist government can concede, it might find support in the ranks of the socialists, but would hardly be one to win over the pure and simple trade unionists. It would appear that Maclean is here again thinking in terms of crises, of clashes with the authorities and a spontaneous uprising on the part of the hungry masses to overthrow the government. This is the contrary of the methods of Lenin and the Bolsheviks, who step by step with their agitation and propaganda, built up an *organisation* in preparation for crisis and clashes, and then formulated, in the very teeth of crises, slogans that corresponded to the immediate practical needs of the working masses, so winning these masses over to the support of that organisation—the Bolshevik Party.

In Scotland there was no such united Party, no vanguard to lead the working class. But let us look at the programme.

The suggested programme consisted of four demands :

(1) A Six Hour Maximum Working Day.
(2) A Minimum Wage of £1 a Day.
(3) Reduction of Prices to Half the Present Level.
(4) Rationing of Work to absorb the unemployed or payment of full wages to the unemployed.

In justification for the demand for a six hour day, reference is made to a standardisation of production, to automatic machinery and extreme sub-division of labour. These, as correctly stated, bring about economies in time, while increasing productivity. And, Maclean urges, the workers ought to benefit by every reduction of the time taken to produce goods. A good socialist argument, supported by the unofficial movements among the workers. But what of the mass of the trade union workers ? In 1919 they struck for a 40 hour week and were beaten. The call for a six hour day would hardly be likely to bring about immediate united action. Here it would appear, Maclean's idealism outstripped his sense of reality.

The arguments adduced in support of the demand for £1 a day, the minimum wage and the reduction of prices by one-half the present level were excellent. Growing profits, high level of prices maintained by the help of the Government, the inflated currency, were all factors in the disparity between wages and the cost of living.

Maclean contended " the Government can, if it chooses, easily reduce prices. It had only to withdraw the Bradburys until the currency has been reduced to about £200 millions and prices at home would fall to at least one-half. . . .

" Should such a course be immediately adopted, Lord Milner in the Lords and A. Chamberlain in the Commons have asserted that a revolution would take place. Were prices to halve, many firms with large supplies of dear raw materials would be unable to sell at the lowered rates and would therefore have to shut down. Capitalism would thus crumple up."

From this Maclean deduced that the demand should go forward for the withdrawal of Bradburys as the first step to reduced prices. And, as the Government to save capitalism cannot yield, so will arise the need to sweep the Government aside.

But this uniform figure for universal application of £1 a day would only appeal and indeed seems to have been intended to appeal to the large sections of the workers as tantamount to a demand for socialism—something no capitalist Government could concede !

On point 4 Maclean is following in the wake of Tom Mann's syndicalist propaganda, *i.e.* for each industry to ration out the work or to maintain at full pay its own quota of unemployed by each industry. But in the capitalist world of planless production and divided craft union interest and working class disunity, it was hardly an immediate fighting demand.

Maclean was serious enough in his desire to secure united action of the official and unofficial movements of the working class. " Every worker," he writes, " understands this programme, powerful unions have already agreed to items 1 and 2, Bob Smillie has centred attention and thought on high prices and Tom Mann is going strong on economic security."

He urged the socialists of the left wing to work through their unions, and through public agitation to force a special labour congress to decide on action for the realisation of the programme. And he ends: " The prosecution of the industrial class war will break the capitalist shell sooner or later."

Whatever may be said about the Programme, Maclean was convinced he had found the basis for unity and for united working class action. Nowhere have we found a more apt expression of the man than in the following terse sentence penned by himself. " The spirit of pessimism and scepticism embodied in the phrase, ' It can't be done,' must be blotted out, and the healthier spirit of optimism and buoyancy expressed in the words, ' It will be done,' must circulate as Labour's new currency." And he set about putting this new currency into circulation.

In June, he writes in the "Vanguard," "Since May Day I have been busy at Airdrie, Coatbridge, Parkhead, Govan, Partick, Clydebank and Dumbarton at the workgates at mid-day and at the usual stances at evening time, arguing the programme and selling ' The Vanguard.' " He proposes to visit Dundee for a week, and then perhaps to return to Greenock, Paisley, Johnstone and Renfrew.

He writes that he is doing all this work largely on his own and arriving everywhere practically unadvertised. He expects soon to have £20 in hand from the sale of his pamphlet, " Condemned from the Dock." With this he intends to issue a leaflet on the Programme, for free distribution to the workers. He had in mind to send petition forms round the works for all to sign asking the trade union federation in engineering and shipbuilding to place it before a special Trade Union Congress with the object of getting the Congress to press the Government. If the Government shuffles, he would have the Congress Parliamentary Committee (there was no General Council of the T.U.C. in those days) given powers to get all the unions to ballot for a general strike. If the officials and executives fail, then the rank and file will be entitled to act on their own through shop committees.

He does not stop here. He writes a letter to the Glasgow Trades Council suggesting a demonstration through the streets and the holding of a Sunday demonstration on Glasgow Green, and puts six points before the Council to protest against :

(1) High and rising prices (bread, coal, rent, etc.), and to demand a special Trades Union Congress to consider action to halve prices.

(2) The Territorial Army recruiting posters on the tramcars.

(3) The occupation of Ireland and the attack on Russia.

(4) The imprisonment of Robert Russell, Winnipeg, by the Canadian Government and the imprisonment of Jim Larkin, Eugene V. Debs, and the thousands of others by the American Government.

(5) The continued starving of Central Europe.

(6) The White Terror in Hungary.

" We shall see," he writes, " if the Trades Council are a lot of auld wives."

Instead of getting any reply from the Trades Council, Maclean says in the next issue of " The Vanguard " that he received a second-hand invitation from W. Regan to speak at an I.L.P. meeting at Nelson's Monument, Glasgow Green."
" I have no objections to such a meeting," he says, " but it is merely a vote-catcher."   " The Trades Council," he insists, " ought to be the fighting centre of Labour in the West of Scotland, and that body ought to have taken action steps." He appeals for some Council members to raise the whole matter.

In the meantime a Conference on the Programme was held in the Central Halls, Bath Street, Glasgow, on 5th June. There it was decided to issue a hundred thousand leaflets explanatory of the programme, " so that at least Scottish Labour can be as consolidated as Irish Labour. . . .   England is bound to follow."

After August 1920 the fight to get the programme accepted by the organised Labour movement disappeared from the pages of " The Vanguard," and would seem to be dissolved in the general propaganda that followed, and in a number of new problems that arose with the formation of the Communist Party of Great Britain in August (1920).

CHAPTER 17

TOWARDS A COMMUNIST PARTY

It is a thousand pities that John Maclean never visited Soviet Russia to see in life, with his own eyes, that revolutionary order which he had been working all his life to establish in Scotland ; and what would have been more valuable, to converse with Lenin and the heroic Bolshevik leaders who had been so successful in the application of Marxist theories. We cannot help thinking that the failure of Maclean to get there is one of the mistakes of his great life. That he had a desire to visit Soviet Russia may be gleaned from the following correspondence. On 10th May, 1920, he writes a letter to Lord Curzon, then Foreign Secretary :

Sir,

I desire you to grant me a permit to visit Russia during the months of July and August, in view of the permits you are granting to Labour and Socialist organisations.

Yours, sincerely,

JOHN MACLEAN.

On 15th May he receives a reply as follows :

Sir,

I am directed by Earl Curzon of Keddlestone to acknowledge the receipt of your letter of the 10th instant, requesting permission to visit Russia during the months of July and August.

Lord Curzon is unable to give a reply to your request at this moment, but if you will apply to him again towards the end of June he will consider whether the necessary facilities can be granted to you or not.

I am, Sir,

Your most obedient servant,

(some undecipherable name).

On the 17th June Maclean again writes :

The Under-Secretary of State,
            Foreign Office,
                    London, S.W.
Sir,

In reply to yours 197172-28 of 15th May, 1920, I wish to re-apply for permission to visit Russia during the months of July and August.

I trust that Lord Curzon will this time reply favourably, in view of the new situation arising out of the Government's negotiations with M. Krassin.

Yours sincerely,
JOHN MACLEAN.

The reply comes back :

" Lord Curzon has given your request his careful consideration, but regrets that he is unable to grant you the necessary facilities."

On 7th July, Maclean tried to get a Pass-port through Thomas Cook's agency, without success, and thereafter relinquished the idea. It was quite unlike the thorough-going class conscious revolutionary that Maclean was to allow legal niceties to hinder him from doing a big job, for certainly no one could dare question Maclean's physical courage. Not only was Soviet Russia looked upon as the vanguard of the world proletarian revolution, but important things were happening there of primary interest to one such as Maclean. The Third International had been formed in March 1919, and its Second Congress, at which all revolutionary trends of thought were invited to be represented, was due to be held in July 1920.

In a world torn and ravaged by four years of war, with the " White " terror raging in some countries, men and women were taking their lives into their own hands to get to the Congress, with no passports or documents of any kind to assist them. It was the duty of the representatives of every revolutionary tendency to be present. Maclean, with others, who were not *persona grata* with Lord Curzon, was invited, and what his Scottish friends were able to do to get there he certainly could have done. But instead of stooping to conquer when it was obvious there was no alternative, he preferred to carry on a forlorn wordy warfare with Lord Curzon.

His absence, however, from the Second Congress of the Third International did not prevent him from accepting its principles. When the 21 conditions of affiliation to the Third International were available he immediately approved of them and published them in " The Vanguard." He recommended and sold the pamphlet published by the left section of the I.L.P., " Moscow's Reply to the I.L.P.," which he regarded as " a pamphlet giving to the world this important statement on the Bolshevik position."

In August 1920 he printed in pamphlet form a special appeal which had been distributed amongst the British soldiers when they occupied Russian territory in 1918-1919, and in big type on the back of one pamphlet he has the following exhortation : " Get the Youths (12-20) to form a Communist League."

Why then, we may ask, did he not take part in the movement for unity and in the formation of the Communist Party of Great Britain which took place in August 1920 ? As we have seen, he had broken with his party, the B.S.P., and was now working on independent lines. He was obsessed by some personal antipathies towards certain leading members of the B.S.P. ; but it would seem that the most important reason for his holding aloof from the unity negotiations was his conviction of the need for a purely Scottish Communist Party.

We have already noted that in his articles he spoke of a Parliament or Soviet of workers for Scotland with headquarters in Glasgow. In the preface to the reproduction of the appeal to British soldiers, above referred to, he says : " I favour a Scottish Communist Republic as a first step towards World Communism, with Glasgow as the head and centre. We must have a Rank and File dictatorship through delegates directly representative of the various workshops and industries. Let then at once a Central Communist Committee be formed in Glasgow, and on with World Revolution."

In an article he wrote at this time he advances reasons why there should be a purely Scottish Communist Party. " Scotland is firmer for Marxism," he writes, " than in any other part of the British Empire, Clyde speakers get bigger and better audiences in Scotland than speakers across the borders with very few exceptions. In other words Scotland is becoming more self-reliant than ever before and looks hopefully for a lead from men reared and trained on this side of the border."

He seized upon Paragraph 17 of the 21 conditions of affiliation to the Third International which laid it down that " Each party must change its old name to that of the Communist Party of such and such a country, section of the Third International." Nothing in this paragraph, Maclean contended, " precludes the formation of a Scottish Party, as Scotland is a definite country," which was true enough.

Meanwhile the elements around the Scottish Workers' Committee movement had formed a Communist Labour Party, and by this time, following the return of William Gallacher from the Second Congress of the Third International, had decided on unity with the C.P.G.B. at a Conference to be held in Leeds in January 1921. Maclean was thus isolated.

The " rump " of the one time active Socialist Labour Party, which had refused all measures of unity, began making advances to Maclean, with a view to winning him over to this camp and Maclean in his honest zeal for a purely Scottish Party coquetted with it. In the December number of " The Vanguard " he writes : " We are summoning by advertisement, not by circular, all in Scotland who favour the gist of the ' Twenty-one Points ' to attend, in person or by delegate, a Conference to form the Scottish Communist Party to represent Marxian Communism in Scotland, or a definite series of groups who will co-operate or amalgamate with the most definitely Marxian organisation in Scotland, the Socialist Labour Party, which fortunately has its headquarters in Glasgow."

This Conference took place on 25th December, 1920, in the S.L.P. Rooms, 50 Renfrew Street, Glasgow, with no material results in the shape of a new Scottish Party. Among those who attended there was no appreciation of the *national* need as understood by Maclean. The " rump " of the S.L.P. had still some slender ties in England, without which it could not survive. On the other hand its narrow sectarianism was in decided contrast to the revolutionary energy of Maclean, who was all for mass action. Hence this Conference was abortive.

Now that a Communist Party had been formed including all

the best left sections and groups of socialists in Scotland, Maclean was completely isolated, save for a few individual followers. At the December Conference in 1920 he had advanced the idea of a Scottish Workers' Republican Party. He now took up this idea and set about propagating the need for such a party. It is no mere conjecture that he was influenced in this direction by the events transpiring in Ireland, for the example of the 1916 Rebellion and of Sinn Fein in setting up its own government in defiance of all the powers of the British Government could not fail to make an impression on Maclean. That it did so, we shall see presently.

CHAPTER 18

BACK IN PRISON

In the meantime nothing could deter Maclean from active public agitation and propaganda, a large place being given in writing and speech to the defence of republican Ireland. He became more and more preoccupied with the situation in Ireland following the Republican successes and the attempts of the British Government to crush the Republic. The repression then conducted in Ireland was the prelude to the disgraceful Black and Tan pogroms and murder campaign. Apart from his natural sympathies with the oppressed Irish people, Maclean was incensed at the pouring of Scots regiments into Ireland to crush the Irish. He wrote a vigorous and terrible indictment of British rule in Ireland, and published it in pamphlet form under the title of " The Irish Tragedy, Scotland's Disgrace," finishing up with an appeal for " A General Strike, for the withdrawal of British troops from Ireland and the release of Jim Larkin."

Fired with the zeal for propaganda and missionary work, and being without a party, Maclean set about gathering together a few trusted friends with the same energy and ambition as himself. In the June 1920 number of " The Vanguard " we find the first reference to a small group of friends as " Our Flying Squad ; The Tramps Trust Unlimited."

This " Flying Squad " consisted of himself, Alexander Ross, Peter Marshall, James D. MacDougall and Harry McShane.

Alexander Ross, or " Big Sandy," as he was familiarly called on account of his personality and stature, was originally a flaxman in the jute industry of Dundee, of which city he was a native. He had been for a time in the Glasgow Police Force, but only for a brief period. During the war he had been a conscientious objector ; after the war he became a public propagandist for the Independent Labour Party in Dundee, where Maclean came into contact with him. Ross had not a profound knowledge of Socialism. but he had a great capacity for telling humorous stories, and provoking an audience to laughter. Maclean invited Ross to assist him, and so he became one of the " Tramps Trust Unlimited."

Peter Marshall was a brother of James Marshall, who, as we have seen, was sent to prison over the assault in Parkhead Forge. Peter had been a conscientious objector during the war and had been in Wakefield Prison. It was here he had come into contact with " Sandy Ross," who now recommended him to Maclean.

Harry McShane was an engineer to trade. He joined the I.L.P., Kingston Branch, Glasgow, in 1909, and in 1910 he responded to the appeal of Victor Grayson in the " Clarion," and joined the British Socialist Party, which was finally constituted in 1911. He was a member of the Provisional Executive of the B.S.P. for Glasgow, and here he met Maclean, who was present as the representative of the South Side Branch.

During the May Day Demonstration on Glasgow Green in 1920, he helped John Maclean to sell the resurrected " Vanguard," and on Maclean's invitation took the chair for the latter at his Sunday evening meetings in Bath Street. This association was kept up until 1922, when Harry was arrested in connection with the eviction fight in South York Street. After seven weeks in prison, and on his release, Harry joined the Communist Party of Great Britain, a step that led to his break with Maclean, who was resolved to have no connection with any " English " organisation. Harry McShane had no part in the setting up of the ephemeral Scottish Workers' Republican Party.

James D. MacDougall, as we have seen, was a companion of John Maclean for a number of years. It is only necessary to say here that MacDougall's health was badly shaken by his prison experience, and when he was again imprisoned for two months in connection with " Tramps Trust " propaganda, he was unable to stand up to the treatment. Attempts were made by the Communist Party to save him for the movement, but without success. He subsequently became connected with the Liberal Party, and from then ceased to have any place in the Socialist movement.

The object of the " Flying Squad " was to tour everywhere with pamphlets and leaflets, to hold public meetings and raise by public collections the funds necessary to spread the propaganda of socialist ideas, and keep the squad flying. Some idea of the kind of work done may be gained from the following propaganda in " The Vanguard " for May 1920 : " Our Flying Squad, ' The Tramps Trust Unlimited,' has done record work this last month at a series of record meetings, all on ' Hands off Ireland.' About forty evening meetings have been held and as many work-gate meetings. Our sales of literature and collections are well over £200.

" We have been busy distributing ' The Labour Programme ' leaflet all over Scotland, and latterly we have disseminated about 100,000 leaflets entitled ' Proposed Irish Massacre,' appealing to Scotsmen not to let themselves be used to murder the Irish race, but to save Ireland if possible by a General Strike, when the Civil War re-starts at Derry or when Lloyd George shuts down the Irish railways."

In September " The Vanguard " writes : " In these months it (The Trust) has published, paid for and distributed almost half a million leaflets. In the same period it has collected and realised off literature sales over £500."

In their campaign in aid of Republican Ireland, the whole " Flying Squad " visited Motherwell on 29th June. Motherwell has a large Irish population, and religious antagonism between Orangemen and Catholics has always been cultivated by interested parties inside and outside the respective churches. While one of the " Squad " was chalking the streets announcing the meeting, its time and place, others were distributing leaflets.

J

During the meeting there was continuous interruption and challenges were being thrown about freely between the speaker (MacDougall) and individuals in the audience.

On the next day, Wednesday, 30th June, Maclean was the speaker. " I walked up and down the main streets of Mother-well for two hours all alone," writes Maclean, " distributing the leaflet, ' Proposed Irish Massacre.' As soon as the meeting opened a crowd of ' orange hooligans ' began interruptions. When he got up to speak he was met with shouts of " Traitor," " Peterhead," " Square-head," and obscene language. The crowd took sides, the Orangemen shouting " Up Derry," the Catholics, " Up Dublin." Throughout this pandemonium Maclean held his ground and kept on speaking, and finished up with a collection of 31/7.

Meanwhile reports came through that a number of crofters in the West Highlands had seized certain lands and defied eviction. The story of this is as follows. In the autumn of 1919 a company was floated by Lord Leverhulme, " The Lewis and Harris Welfare and Development Limited," with a capital of £2,000,000. The purpose of the company was stated to be the " Business of Concessionnaires and Manufacturers." To prepare the way for the company it was decided to clear the islands of Harris, Lewis and St. Kilda of the crofters, many of whom were newly demobilised ex-servicemen. The reply of the crofters was to seize certain farms and to squat on them.

The claim of the crofters was set forth in a letter sent to the Secretary for Scotland dated 11th August, 1920. There it was stated that " the whole of the farm of Gress, of parts of which we have been in occupation for a considerable time past, was scheduled for small holdings before the commencement of the war ; and the scheme would have been carried out but for the war, which resulted in all such schemes being suspended for the time being."

The crofters alleged they did not demur at the time, being called upon to volunteer for the army. During the recruiting campaign they were told how ready the Government would be to recognise the loyalty of the crofters by giving them the use of the land.

When the Leverhulme Company bought the Islands it had known that the Gress Farm was scheduled for small holdings.

Thus the crofters Acts were to be wiped out by the stroke of a millionaire's pen. " We say to the Government : Honour your bond without fear or favour."

The " Tramps Trust " decided to send Sandy Ross and Peter Marshall to Stornoway. Only Ross was able to get there and he managed to see and speak with the crofters who had seized the Gress Farm. Maclean meanwhile had gone to Dublin, as he said, " to establish an *entente* between the Celts of Scotland and the Celts of Ireland, and to further my efforts to prevent Scottish boys being used by England to murder Irish boys."

On returning from Dublin, Maclean decided to make the journey to Stornoway and to see things for himself. He visited the Coll Raiders and spoke with the crofters. At Stornoway, on 4th August, he addressed a public meeting on behalf of the raiders, defending them against Leverhulme and urging unity and support for the crofters. He brought back a copy of the aforementioned appeal sent to the Secretary for Scotland (" the Highland traitor " said Maclean, " who got me a three years sentence for resisting the Conscription Act of the Germans of England ") and published it in " The Vanguard."

Maclean was of the opinion that this clearing of the Islands had the more sinister and far-reaching motive—that of preparing harbours and docks for war with the United States, which he was convinced was to be the next clash of arms, arising from the conflict between these two imperialist powers, and now rendered inevitable after the defeat of Germany. When, subsequently, through the intervention of the Government, the crofters were persuaded to give up the farms, Maclean declared, " It looks as if the people had sold their son's lives for a mess of pottage. Their only salvation lies in the Workers' Revolution since revolution alone can avert the next great clash of Empires."

It certainly was no fault of Maclean that the Highland crofters are still faced with the problem of landlordism. It is not without significance that one of the last acts of the son of Daniel Maclean, the crofter, should be in defence of the crofters' interests.

But there were other problems equally as distracting as the Irish situation and the highland clearances. Unemployment was now raising its ugly head and becoming a serious problem in Glasgow as elsewhere. As the autumn came and the winter of 1920 approached, Maclean threw himself into the organisation of the unemployed with his customary ardour. A meeting was convened and deputations were elected to wait on the Town Council and the Trades and Labour Council. The Town Council received the deputations and a series of demands were presented. The deputations demanded :

(1) Food at municipal restaurants as the most urgent question of all.
(2) Work on farm colonies at trade union rates of pay, with representation on all committees employing the unemployed.
(3) Houses to shelter full families in the colonies.
(4) All available new and repair work of the Corporation to be proceeded with as a matter of urgency.
(5) Failing work, emigration to Russia.
(6) The use of the City Hall, in which the unemployed could meet to discuss its problems.

Maclean, in writing about these activities, says : " We have found up-to-date every Committee willing to convene a special meeting to discuss matters with us."

It was agreed to grant the use of the City Hall three times a week. The heads of Departments were convened to get work under way.

The Restaurant Committee, the Distress Committee, the Education authority, etc., were convened to meet. Says Maclean : " Never before in the history of Glasgow has such alacrity been shown." " And why ? " he asks. " Because our committee appears every day lobbying Labour Councillors and others on every issue."

In London the unemployed had come into conflict with the police, and in Coventry the unemployed had attempted to seize some works. Maclean opposed such means at this juncture. " To rush a works just now," he says, " would mean split heads and a defeat for the Labour Candidates. A Labour Council," he declared, " would respond to pressure more readily than a bourgeois one. If Labour failed then a forceful revolutionary fight was the logical next stage. . . . We mean to exhaust every constitutional method of safeguarding the unemployed of our class," he says, " and whatever happens after that we certainly will not be to blame."

His stand for the unemployed again brought him into conflict with the police, this time at Airdrie, where he had been in the habit of addressing meetings for some time. With his colleague, Sandy Ross, he visited Airdrie and addressed a meeting at the corner of Hallcraig on 30th April, 1921. The Chief Constable, a police-sergeant and a constable were present at the meeting and notes were taken. Maclean spoke on his familiar theme, the general strike, revolution and the role of the army and navy. He denounced the Middle Class Union and the Government for their behaviour during the miners' lock-out on 1st April, 1921. Both Maclean and Ross were subsequently arrested and charged with sedition. Bail was granted, and they stood trial at Airdrie Sheriff Court on 17th May, 1921.

Once more he defended himself, using the court as a tribune to address the people. He spoke for seventy minutes in his defence. The Fiscal only occupied five minutes in demanding a conviction. Both prisoners were found guilty and sentenced to three months imprisonment. An additional penalty of £20 fine was imposed on Sandy Ross, with the alternative of another three months. The fine was paid, and Ross was released. He came out of prison and seized the first opportunity to repeat the speech he had made at Airdrie. He was again arrested and sentenced to four months in prison.

Maclean was released in August 1921, and immediately took up the agitation for the release of Sandy Ross. He came straight from Barlinnie Prison to the Central Police Court to give evidence on behalf of Harry McShane and Duffy, who had been charged with breaking a bye-law by selling on Glasgow Green a pamphlet, " Karl Liebknecht : His Work and Message."

On 13th September he addressed a meeting at Dunmore Street, Gorbals, Glasgow. At this meeting he said :

" I stand on the same platform as Sandy Ross, and as long as I am a free man, I will say the same—that is, if you cannot get food in a constitutional way, I say, take it."

The following week he was arrested, charged with sedition on account of this utterance, and remitted to the Glasgow

Sheriff Court to be tried by Sheriff Boyd. Prior to the trial, as Maclean himself relates, " I went on hunger strike for eighteen days before Dr. Garry forcibly fed me in presence of Dr. Walter of Barlinnie, as a protest against detention prior to trial."

Once more he defended himself and his convictions unflinchingly. " I said, so far as we were concerned, if it was a case of death by starvation, or the taking of food, I urged the taking of food rather than death by starvation ; and from that I will not recoil.

" During the war it was said John Maclean was traitor to his country, I never was. I never said I would fight for my country, I said I would fight for my class.

" When I stand up for my comrade I am prepared to suffer for him. I am glad I have been charged here, because it is going to let the whole world know that John Maclean stands by those who are of the same convictions as himself. This is a glorious opportunity for me and I am proud that I have been indicted for standing by Sandy Ross—for standing by my class. . . . I, for one, am out for a Scottish Workers' Republic." He was sentenced to twelve months' imprisonment, which he served in Barlinnie Prison, Glasgow. Unfortunately, Maclean's loyalty to Ross was not reciprocated. While Maclean was in Barlinnie Sandy Ross was released. On his release he publicly declared he was finished. Subsequently he went to work in India, where he died. With the loss of MacDougall and Ross, " The Tramps Trust " faded out and Maclean became more isolated than ever.

This term of imprisonment for Maclean is noteworthy for the fact that for the first time he forced the authorities to concede to him the status of political prisoner. He received his own food, handed to him personally from outside three times a day. He got papers and books. He even got, on his demand, an unexpurgated edition of Lord Byron's works ; a demand we may presume made as a challenge to bourgeois orthodoxy and authority. The recognition of the status of political prisoner, however, was a valuable precedent from which future politicals may profit.

From Barlinnie Prison Maclean sent out two letters to his old friend and comrade Hugh Hinshelwood. From these letters we get a glimpse of the things then occupying his mind, in particular his preoccupation with study class work.

In the first letter dated 13th February, 1922, he acknowledges receipt of Hinshelwood's note proposing to visit him, and goes on, " might I suggest a class again in Greenock in some bright and central hall, like the Central Halls, Glasgow, for instance. The C.P. or the Trades' Council might be induced to run it along with you, or merely by advertisement in the ' Telegraph,' etc. The last class I had there was a huge success."

" Six weeks will see me free again, and between this and then I have as much reading as will keep me going. I see we missed £250 at the T.U.C. Better luck elsewhere, I trust."

In the second letter, dated 16th October, 1922, he thanks Hinshelwood for his efforts *re* the Greenock class, and says : " I'll accept all arrangements made by you cheerfully, since you know the situation and I don't. But just one point, since I saw you the Unemployed Committee in K.P. (Kinning Park) write me asking if I'd again stand for the Town Council. I've consented. The election is on Tuesday, 7th November. Although my name has illegally been deleted from the voters' roll and *may not* be re-inserted, thus debarring me from standing, I'll still hold meetings in the ward. So, therefore, if you could defer the opening till Wednesday, 8th November, and run the class the last Wednesday of December, that would suit me best. Of course, if your arrangement can't be altered, I'll come all right on Wednesday, 1st November, as by choice I'd rather teach than ' orate ' on purely local issues, important though these be. So thus again, with this one further request, I leave you to go ahead."

His mind is also working on the unemployed question, for in this same letter he goes on to say : " Perhaps you could get into touch with Geddes and see if the Unemployed Committee would organise a mass meeting of the unemployed (not on relief work) every Wednesday afternoon when I could give some lectures on Economics and Industrial History—perhaps, simpler and more dilute than the evening ones. If some local comrade would help me by taking up the Industrial History and I think Geddes could find one competent, that would relieve my voice afternoon and evening and leave me fresher for the more exacting lectures on Economics. It would also be good for the one taking the History (both afternoon and evening, if possible). Of course, I'd like him to work with me by arranging his lectures to cover the field I'd discuss with him."

And he concludes : " Do you remember the unemployed campaign of 'Xmas 1905, I think, when I urged the recovery of Mearns Moor ? Well, then, I'm making that the centre of my demands for the unemployed at this juncture. I've got good maps here, and now I'm going to look them up so as to get ready for the fray. Till I see you, best wishes."

In accordance with Maclean's request the local friends secured the use of the Saloon in the Town Hall in Greenock, which was and is used for receptions, etc. All arrangements were made for the class, fees fixed, etc. But John's unbounded enthusiasm for a successful enterprise led to unforeseen developments.

He came to Greenock that afternoon and anticipated all the arrangements requested by himself, by getting into touch with one or two friends who were out of work. He organised a demonstration of the unemployed who were willing to come to his class in the evening. He so timed things that the demonstration arrived at the Town Hall about the time for opening the doors. Those who had been previously enrolled and paid their fees found themselves at a disadvantage in the crowd that surged into the Saloon.

Such an incident reveals in Maclean his tremendous urge to get to the masses.

CHAPTER 19

LAST DAYS

ON 23rd October, 1922, Maclean was released, and immediately plunged into the General Election campaign in the Gorbals, where he was again a candidate. Speaking in the St. Mungo Hall, Glasgow, on 19th November, 1922, he denounced General Smuts for the execution of Long, Hull and Lewis in connection with the Rand strike in South Africa, and denounced Cosgrove for the execution of the Irish Republicans.

But the situation this time in the Gorbals was entirely different from 1918. To quote Maclean's own words : " I came out of prison in debt, had no committee and had no arrangements, and yet I stood." Yet, even though he was isolated it was only after much difficulty that the Labour Party leadership succeeded in getting a candidate to stand against him. They ultimately found one in the patternmaker and I.L.P.er, George Buchanan, who not having been discredited in the eyes of the workers, as had Barnes, and having flirted with the unofficial movement during the war, was a more acceptable candidate to the Divisional Labour Party.

In his first electioneering appeal Maclean declares : " I stand in the Gorbals and before the world as a bolshevik, alias a communist, alias a revolutionist, alias a Marxist. My symbol is the Red Flag, and it I shall always keep floating on high." After recounting his record from the outbreak of war in 1914, he gives a restatement of principles, and concludes with the declaration : " To get a Scottish Workers' Republic I shall not go to the London House of Commons, but stay in Scotland, helping the unemployed, standing by those at work, educating in the Scottish Labour College and carrying revolutionary propaganda all over Scotland. " If you cannot agree with me, then vote for George Buchanan, the representative of the Labour Party. On no account vote for anyone else." There is a curious blend here of Irish Sinn Fein and class loyalty to the Labour Party.

There were four candidates for the Gorbals in this election : Maclean, described as Communist ; Buchanan, Labour ; Harper, National Labour ; and Robertson, Liberal. The results of the polling were : Labour, 16,479 ; National Labour, 8,276 ; Communist, (Maclean) 4,027 ; and the Liberal, 1,456. The Gorbals remained overwhelmingly Labour, but Maclean's stock had fallen by nearly 50 per cent. compared to the election in 1918.

Undaunted, he continued to carry on his agitation and propaganda. While he was in Barlinnie Prison he had read in the press of the tragic death of an ex-soldier and unemployed worker in the Southern Police Station, Glasgow. The report seemed to suggest foul play, and Maclean was convinced in his own mind that the police had killed this man. As soon as he was released he collected the newspaper reports, spoke with the widow and the solicitor and sent copies of the special post-mortem examination to the Prime Minister and to the Glasgow Labour group of M.P.s, demanding compensation for the widow. Subsequently, he published the story and correspondence as an exposure of what he called the " Glasgow Police Murder Hush-up."

Maclean was convinced in the light of his own experience, and of what he had seen and heard in prison, that the police often resorted to measures of force and violence against spirited prisoners ; and he was determined to vindicate his allegations against the police, and, as he said in his " Exposure," " to rouse the masses of the people so that in future the police will be the servants of the common people and not their brutal tyrants."

During the spring and summer of 1923 he continued his propaganda meetings and activity on behalf of the unemployed. The parliamentary elections of 1922 left unsettled the political situation in the country, and another general election was fixed to take place on Thursday, 6th December, 1923. Again Maclean stood as candidate for the Gorbals Division, but this time as a Republican, the nominee of the new Scottish Workers Republican Party, which he had formed.

In this election address he gave a restatement of his views which merits quoting at length, since this proved to be the last he ever made. He takes as his starting point Baldwin's policy. He denies the claim of Baldwin that a high tax on foreign goods and a lower one, or none at all, on colonial goods, will help the colonies, revive industry here and help the unemployed. Imperial trade preference can but pull the empire more closely together for a bigger and bloodier war than the last.

He reminds his readers how he had tried to impress upon them at the last election the importance of the Pacific Ocean Conference called by the United States, which he claims was to lay the basis of American supremacy in the Far East markets, and how Bonar Law sought to counter the move of the United States with the Imperial Trade Conference, declaring that England's only assured markets were in the colonies.

Maclean then summarises his interpretation of development as follows : " I see America aspiring to command not only the Asiatic markets, but also those of America as well. I see America's ally, France, pinning down England in Europe, and gathering allies and strength to capture the Near East, Mediterranean and African markets. I see England in desperation gathering her imperial resources together for a dying kick in the form of a war with America for supremacy in the Pacific Ocean. . . .

" The root of all the trouble in society at present," he declares, " is the inevitable robbery of the workers by the propertied class, simply because it is the propertied class. To end that robbery would be to end the social troubles of modern society. The way to end that robbery is the transfer of the land and means of production and transport from the present possessors to the community. Community ownership is communism The transfer is a social revolution, not the bloodshed that may or may not accompany the transfer."

From this he passes on to his policy in the Election. "Russia could not produce the World Revolution. Neither can we in the Gorbals, in Scotland, in Great Britain. Before England is ready I am sure the next war will be on us. I, therefore, consider that Scotland's wisest policy is to declare for a Republic in Scotland, so that the youths of Scotland will not be forced out to die for England's markets.

" I accordingly stand out as a Scottish Republican candidate feeling sure that if Scotland had to elect a Parliament to sit in Glasgow, it would vote for a working class Parliament . . . the social revolution is possible sooner in Scotland than in England.

" If Baldwin's capitalist policy is to bind the Empire closer together to fight American capitalism, and incidentally keep the workers enslaved, then the working class policy ought to be to break up the Empire to avert war and enable the workers to triumph in every country and colony. Scottish separation is part of the process of England's Imperial disintegration and is a help towards the ultimate triumph of the workers of the world."

" This policy of a Workers' Republic in Scotland," he insists, " debars me from going to John Bull's London Parliament. . . . Had the Labour men stayed in Glasgow and started a Scottish

Parliament, as did the genuine Irish in Dublin in 1918, England would have sat up and made concessions to Scotland just to keep her ramshackle Empire intact to bluff other countries."

In conclusion, he declares, "neither Free Trade nor Protection is of use to the workers. Taxation of land or capital, including the Capital Levy, is of no use to the workers. No housing or other social reform is really possible whilst industry is paralysed and the earnings of the workers are ever shrinking. The only possible hope is community ownership of the means of production. . . . Every vote cast against me is one cast for World War and the further starvation of the world's workers. Every vote cast for me is for World Peace and Eternal Economic Security for the human family."

It would be futile to-day to condemn Maclean because things did not happen as he thought they would. France *was* in 1923 seeking to establish her hegemony in Europe. The United States *was* reaching out to the markets in the East, while raising higher the tariff walls in her home market. And Maclean was not alone in believing that war between America and Britain was certain, as may be gleaned from the political writings and speeches of the period. That events subsequently were to take another course is no reflection upon Maclean's judgment in 1923.

He is on firmer ground when he is dealing with the root of all the troubles in present day society, and the way to end them. His contention that social reforms were not really possible whilst industry is paralysed was to have striking confirmation five years later when the country was in the grip of a general crisis.

As to the wisdom or otherwise of proclaiming at this juncture for "separation" and his determination to follow the example of the Irish Republicans and not go to Westminster, if elected, and his belief that "the social revolution is possible sooner in Scotland than in England," there is much room to differ. This was not the real Maclean speaking, but a man who had suffered much, and who was no longer seeing things in their proper perspective, due to the warping of his better judgment. What was permanent, and will redound to his lasting credit, was his incorruptibility and unshakeable belief in the social revolution—the final victory of the working class.

This election address was issued on 23rd November, 1923, but he was not fated to go to the poll. He was already a very sick man, and ought to have been receiving proper care and attention. Instead, he was to be found speaking at out-door meetings, day and night, regardless of inclement weather, denying himself the comfort and quiet that he deserved after passing through such strenuous times. Alas, his domestic circumstances deranged, those political friends who had gathered around him seemed oblivious to the tragic situation to which this once sturdy vigorous man was reduced, and he got no rest. Seized with a virulent attack of pneumonia, he died two days later on 30th November, 1923, six days before Polling Day. Thus passed away, literally in harness, one of Scotland's most heroic, courageous revolutionary fighters and defenders of the cause of the working class, which he held to be the cause of all humanity.

The " Greenock Telegraph " reported on 3rd December, " So large was the audience in the Town Hall at a Communist demonstration on Saturday evening (1st December) that the doors had to be closed shortly after the start. The " Telegraph said : " Mr. Hugh Hinshelwood, Gourock, made a fitting reference to the death of Mr. John Maclean, the Glasgow Communist, which had struck him with more poignancy than anything for many years. No one had undergone more agony and torture for the cause than had Mr. Maclean.

" A touching incident followed. On the invitation of Mr. Hinshelwood the massed audience rose to their feet, doffed their caps, and had a moment's silence to the memory of Mr. Maclean and his work."

On a bleak December day thousands of workers marshalled at Eglinton Toll, Glasgow, to mark their respect for the dead warrior. Forming into line four abreast the long concourse of mourners marched to Auldhouse Street where workers had been passing by the bier all day. The concourse fell in behind the carriage that bore the last remains to Eastwood Cemetery, where now a simple stone marks the last resting place with the letters inscribed in bold type—MACLEAN.

CHAPTER 20

WORKING CLASS EDUCATION

IT is, above all else, with the problem of working class education that the name of John Maclean is associated. A study of
his life would therefore be incomplete without a more detailed
survey of his strenuous activities in this field.

The serious worker who sets out to become an educated man
needs more than general academic and technical education.
He needs also such instruction as will serve him as armament
in the struggle of his class under capitalism. The bourgeoisie
has tried to discredit the " class " education of the workers. It
has no objection to the workers equipping themselves in the
technique of their job. Indeed, it is keen on promoting technical education, mostly, of course, at public expense. But for
the workers to study the history of the origin of classes, the
economic relations between wage-labour and capital, and the
social sciences generally—that is anathema. In the eyes of the
good bourgeois this breeds " bad citizens," destroys that
" social unity," which in his eyes is so desirable, directly
threatens his own power and philosophy. He who would
concentrate upon working class education of the kind referred
to is an enemy of society.

The movement in the direction of conscious working class
education, began to take shape in the decade prior to the birth
of John Maclean. It got its impulse from the numerous
Mechanics' Institutes, Working Men's Clubs and Adult Schools
peculiar to England. Scotland had no such institutions. As
far back as 1800 a " Working Men's College " was founded in
London by a bourgeois philanthropist, Frederick Maurice. At
this college, University men lectured in their spare time. In
1867 the University Extension movement was started in
Cambridge.

In 1874, at the 6th Trade Union Congress, held at Sheffield,
Alexander Macdonald, the Scottish miners' leader, offered a
prize on " The history and vocation of Trade Unions, their
relations with Trade, and their advantage to members."

The newly founded socialist societies in the " 80's " of the
last century gave an impetus to the movement. The Fabians

began lecturing to the working men's clubs on elementary political economy, and the industrial history of the nineteenth century.

The Social Democratic Federation began the diffusion of a new literature drawn from the teachings of Marx and Engels, and from which economic study classes sprung up wherever a group of social democrats came together.

In 1887, Thorold Rogers, the famous radical bourgeois Professor in Oxford, was giving lectures in Industrial and Commercial History that were radical in their content. A few years later H. de B. Gibbons in 1896 published his " Industry in England." Both these authors became very popular in the study classes, and helped the working class students to gain a wide knowledge of economics and industrial history.

In 1899, two Americans, Walter Vrooman and Dr. C. Beard, advanced funds to start a Working Men's College at Oxford, which became known as the Ruskin College. The college was owned by them. The governing body was appointed from University men and trade union leaders. The parliamentary Committee of the T.U.C. delegated George N. Barnes of the Engineers, James Sexton and Ben Tillet of the Dockers, to represent the T.U.C. on the governing Board.

In 1903 Mr. Albert Mansbridge, together with a group of Trade Unionists and Co-operators, secured the good-will and assistance of the Universities and arranged for a Conference at Oxford, representative of both the Universities and working class organisations. From this Conference was formed the Workers' Educational Association.

Some students at Ruskin, becoming dissatisfied with the kind of teaching they were getting, began to form classes among themselves in those subjects they were primarily interested. In 1908 these students formed the Plebs' League, and in 1909, on the dismissal of their Principal, Denis Hird, the students went on strike, and the Central Labour College was formed.

The first trade union organisation to support financially the C.L.C. was the Monmouth Valleys District of the South Wales Miners' Federation. In 1916 the S.W.M.F. and the N.U.R. finally completed negotiations for the purchase and control of the College.

Simultaneously with these developments in England a network of study circles was being built up by the Social Democrats in Scotland.   In Glasgow, the stone breaker William Nairne, supported by Robert Hutchison and Donald Stewart, was propounding the economic doctrines of Karl Marx at public meetings on Glasgow Green, and at study circles within the local Branch rooms of the S.D.F.

The work of Nairne, who died in 1901, was carried on by a younger generation in the S.D.F. and with greater intensity in the Socialist Labour Party after the split in 1903.   Classes in political economy, industrial history, logic, grammar and public speaking, were held in Glasgow, Falkirk, Leith, Edinburgh, Kirkcaldy and Aberdeen.   When, therefore, John Maclean joined the S.D.F. he inherited a rich tradition in working class education based on Marxism.   It remained for him to open out new fields of endeavour.   This he did on a wide scale, and adopted a more popular method of teaching.

The method of Nairne, Yates and the earlier tutors was intense and in a large measure scholastic.   This method was alien to the temperament and disposition of Maclean.   A born agitator, he sought to connect practice with theory.   Having first expounded the theoretical laws from Marx's " Capital," he would cite quotations often brought to him by his students, from the current press, or speeches of politicians and professors, link these up with the political orientation of the government of the day and thus seek to guide the listeners towards action.

From a series of Notes for lectures given during the war 1914-18 by John Maclean at the B.S.P. (Glasgow) Economic and Industrial History Class, I have chosen the following " Lecture V " as a good example to illustrate the manner in which he sought to popularise a highly technical subject.

NOTES OF LECTURES GIVEN BY JOHN MACLEAN AT THE B.S.P. (GLASGOW) ECONOMIC AND INDUSTRIAL HISTORY CLASS.

LECTURE V

Two commodities—*Labour Power* and *Gold*—deserve special examination and discussion.

Labour Power is stored-up human energy. This, the worker sells for a wage. It is wrong to state that the worker sells his *Labour*. We have seen that the capitalist uses every device to squeeze as much *Labour* out of the worker as possible. At the same time he tries to pay as low a *Wage* as possible. If he paid for *Labour*, these opposing pressures of maximum output at minimum wages would not be needed.

Wage is the money exchange value or *Price* of Labour Power.

Wages rise and fall in obedience to the law of Supply and Demand. For facts, see " Riches and Poverty," and the " Labour Gazette." When a trade boom comes trade unions push for increase of wages : when a crisis comes masters' unions enforce a reduction of wages.

Wages are determined ultimately by the Law of Value. Value is the labour-time needed to make a commodity. Labour Power is not directly created by Labour, but by food, clothing, shelter, education, etc. The time needed to make the commodities required to keep a man in efficiency, as well as his wife and three children, fixes the Value of Labour Power.

Account must be taken of the strength or skill required, regularity of work, social customs, trade organisation, etc. These factors explain differences of wages from trade to trade, from country to country, and between " skilled " and " unskilled " workers.

In the long run " Piece " and " time " wages work out to an equality, owing to the fluidity of labour.

The greater the Value of the necessaries of life the greater the Value of Labour Power : the lower the commodity Value the lower the Labour Power Value, or the greater the output of wealth the smaller the share received by the workers and the greater the share seized by the " shirkers."

The higher that Prices rise, the higher must Wages go. Facts prove that Prices may rise and Wages fall, and that Prices may fall and Wages rise. This shows that Prices and Wages are not necessarily dependent on one another, as is so frequently asserted. In the long run these contrary tendencies cancel one another to yield the first result.

K

Experience shows that the workers' wages just about keep
them going. Their savings are about £600,000,000. Only
a small number possess this. The others' debts are not
tabulated, but they perhaps equal the savings when
starvation is added to money debts.

Those who may save are the unmarried, the married without
children, the married after the family is self-supporting,
foremen, managers, etc.

Bad times, big families, irregular work, ill-health, accident, or
death may eat up savings and induce debts.

Employers, knowing the temporary advantage of strict
domestic economy on the part of workers, have always
insisted on the workers practising " thrift " " abstinence,"
" savings," etc. The recent labour unrest (1911-1913) saw
strenuous attempts in America and elsewhere to get the
workers' wives to cook cheap but energy-creating dishes.
The war has induced a full blast of " thrift " preaching,
cheap recipes, and economy cookery classes (all for the
workers).

Workers bargain about wages on the " cost of living."

The propertied class feel virtuous when keeping wages low, for
otherwise, the workers would drink and make beasts of
themselves. The work done is lost sight of.

Capitalists have experimented with lunatics, paupers, soldiers,
navvies, etc., to find out the minimum cost producing
maximum efficiency. Physiologists have helped them.
For a moderate day's work 3,500 calories of energy must
be in the worker's food. Of sixty working class families
examined in Glasgow in 1911-1912 by D. E. Lindsay, the
average was 3,163 calories per man. About a third were
suffering from starvation.

Unemployment, chronic and spasmodic, prevents wages being
forced much above the subsistence level. A Wages Fund
is a capitalist myth.

The foregoing are only the " Notes." The reader can imagine
the scope each of these points would give to a lecturer like
Maclean, armed with press cuttings and references, and eager to

expose " capital " and the employing class. It is not surprising that his audience ran into three figures ; the class-room was transformed into a propagandist lecture.

An ardent co-operator, Maclean utilised to the full the possibilities afforded by the Educational Department of the Co-operative Societies. A few days before he went to his Trial in April 1916 he sent out the following circular letter :

Dear Comrade,

I am writing to you on a matter of importance and would like to enlist your support. Our comrade, NEIL MACLEAN, has been nominated for the Scottish Section of the Co-operative Union by the following Societies, Kinning Park, St. Rollox, Clydebank, and Leith Provident. The Scottish Section is the Committee which has the organising of the Educational and Propaganda affairs of the Co-operative movement in Scotland, and there are also two of its members on the Parliamentary Committee. When I mention the fact that the Societies in Scotland vote the sum of £19,000 ANNUALLY for their Educational Committee you will realise the power for good that such a body can become. NEIL MACLEAN'S views are well enough known and it will be unnecessary for me to indicate his policy, if elected. If you are on the Committee of the local society, or know anyone who is, you will be doing a favour if you will use what influence you possess to get the local Society to vote for him. There are ten men elected every year and the Societies can vote for ten, but if they only vote for one they cannot give him the votes they withhold from the other candidates. Thus if the Society has four votes, the four votes can be given to each of the ten men as there are ten places to fill, if the Society decides to vote for one man only it can only give him four votes. The Voting papers will be issued in the course of the next two or three weeks, so that it is time to get ready for the election.

Thanking you in anticipation for any assistance you can give.

Yours fraternally,

JOHN MACLEAN.

Under their auspices he lectured to a large audience of co-operators in different parts of the country. His Co-operative engagements fulfilled, he spoke at public meetings on behalf of the local branches of the Socialist Party.

Since he was a school teacher the long summer vacation enabled him in this way to travel extensively up and down the country, teaching and lecturing.

When war broke out there was no more popular socialist figure in the country thanks to his energetic activity spread over the many years since joining the Social Democratic Federation. There were few important towns or mining villages in which the name of John Maclean was not known—Maclean the symbol of revolutionary socialism.

The outbreak of war in no way interrupted the general educational work on the Clydeside. On the contrary the urge among the workers, towards reading, study and propaganda steadily increased. In addition to the classes held at week-ends, mostly on Sunday forenoon, classes in Marxian Economics and in Industrial History began to be formed in the workshops. They were held during the dinner-hour in the day-time ; and during the break in the night-shift between the hours of one to two a.m. There was no centralisation in this work. It was largely spontaneous and unco-ordinated, and limited in scope only by the lack of teachers.

By the end of 1915 the question was raised by John Maclean as to the necessity of forming a Scottish Labour College, and a Conference was arranged for this purpose. 500 delegates attended from trade union, co-operative and socialist organisations. This, the first Conference to establish a Scottish Labour College, was held on Saturday, 12th February, 1916, in the Co-operative Hall, Clarence Street, Glasgow. It was held two days before Maclean was released from the Magistrates' Court pending his trial before the Sheriff. The opening address, intended to be given by Maclean, was not quite finished. It was completed in its final form and read by James D. Mac-Dougall in the absence of Maclean. Bob Smillie presided at the Conference.

The following extracts from his plea for a Labour College for Scotland will give the reader some idea of the scope of working class education as conceived by Maclean :

" It is my hope that you delegates will become just as aware as the masters are of the need for specific forms of education. The State provides an elementary and higher education that certainly needs purging and overhauling ; the State may now be willing to enforce a technical or commercial training on every boy and girl not intending to enter the professions ; but the State, because it must be a Capitalist State so long as Capitalism endures, will not provide a full education to equip workers to carry on the working class movement or the fight for the ending of Capitalism itself.

In consequence, I am firmly convinced that the workers must establish and maintain their own Colleges to equip themselves for their own specific tasks as a class.

Many of the older Trade Union officials and leaders may be dubious as to the need for the establishment of a College lest there should emerge from it rivals for the positions they hold. But a slight consideration of the vast problems and difficulties that the resumption of peace will raise for solution ought to show the need for a rapidly growing number of men able to defend the rights of the workers and enable them to proceed towards the full control of industry in a thoroughly disciplined fashion.

More and better-trained organisers of the industrial workers are absolutely necessary in the future. I have no desire to belittle the ability and capacity of men who, like Mr. Robert Smillie, have received their training in the rough-and-tumble world of hard experiences. But I believe that he would be the very first to admit that, with a sound working class education, he could have rendered even greater service to our class than we all too gladly admit he has given in his strenuous and eventful career.

More and better working class papers and magazines are needed, if the people are going to get facts instead of fiction, working class instead of Capitalist leading articles. The men to conduct and write for these papers must likewise be trained.

The next source of opposition to a Labour College will be the Curriculum. In the city where Adam Smith discoursed on the " Wealth of Nations," a full century-and-a-half ago, it should hardly be necessary to insist that the principal study ought to be Economics. I fancy we are largely agreed on that. The

difficulty arises as to the kind of Economics. At a Labour
College Economics must be taught fundamentally from the
Labour standpoint. Otherwise we ought to send our students
to the capitalist Universities. Our students must make the
writings of Marx and Marxian scholars the basis of their
studies ; otherwise the College becomes an expensive tragedy.
That does not imply the exclusion of the study of Marshall ;
the pontiff of present-day capitalist Economics, or the other
great writers who have influenced or are to-day moulding
economic thought.

Just as economics must be studied from the working class
point of view, so must history. A Labour College must, of
course, provide for the teaching of Industrial History, just
as has been done in the various Sunday and Evening Classes
held hitherto. But useful as such a study may be, it is not
sufficient. If we confined ourselves to Industrial History our
students would get merely one-sided views of the events of the
past. However much we may be inclined to admire the work
of the economic historians—such as Rogers, Ashley, Cunning-
ham, De Gibbins, etc.—we cannot afford to forget that what
we get from them is but partial history after all. They teach
the history of the development of technique from primitive
tools of rough stone to the latest electrically-driven machines,
and of economic association from the manor to the modern
factory, and the information they furnish is essential, but it
only concerns some of the facts of life.

The most effective method of historical explanation is
undoubtedly the materialistic method of Marx, whereby we
rise from an understanding of the mode of production prevailing
at a certain epoch, to a knowledge of the reasons for the origin
and decay of classes and their antagonism to one another. The
State and its functions are explained, and political struggles are
seen to be at bottom class struggles. The law is found to be
the expression of the interests of the dominant class in the
State. Changes in the morality and in the ideas held by men
are found to be due to an altered economic environment.
Transformation of the methods of wealth production is seen to
be the necessary outcome of the biologic will to live. By means
of this method, then, we can understand history, and ade-

quately explain it. History ceases to be a happy hunting ground for either simple narrators or purveyors of romance.

Naturally the curriculum would devote special attention to the history of Trade Unionism. And what better training could students get than to be set to do research work into the history of their own Union or the particular group to which it belonged.

The development of the Co-operative movement would require to be one of the subjects of special study. It is only in recent days, one might say, that the barriers separating the Co-operative from the general Labour movement have been broken down. Trade Unionists and Socialists are only beginning to realise what they have lost in failing to utilise the assistance of this powerful auxiliary. The position of dignified isolation, formerly taken up by the Co-operative movement, is giving place to co-operation with other working class forces. The essential unity of the working class movement, under all its different forms, is a conception that is very prevalent to-day.

Such general educational subjects as English, Composition, and Literature, Arithmetic and Algebra, would also demand attention. Students could receive a training in public speaking and debate such as would save them much time later on, when they came to play their part in the movement.

That there is need for a College is proved by the success which has attended the voluntary classes, handicapped as the students are by long hours of toil, and by the size of this Conference to-day. The idea is certainly in the air. It is our hope that this meeting to-day may prove to be the beginning of a movement which will bring the idea down to earth, and have it embodied in reality. The capitalists feel the need of theoretical and scientific training for themselves, if they are to successfully compete, by greater exploitation of the workers against America and Germany when the war is over. The workers, if they are successfully to resist increased exploitation, and to make progress towards freedom, can only do so if they utilise their resources wisely for the training of leaders and the diffusion of essential knowledge amongst themselves."

After the discussion on the address, the following resolution moved by Thomas Scott, Kinning Park Co-operative Educational Committee, and seconded by William McCreath, District Committee of the A.S.E., was unanimously passed ;

" That this Conference of delegates from labour organisations in Scotland approves of the establishment of a Scottish Labour College, and agrees to the appointment of a Provisional Committee with full powers to act until the First Annual Conference of the Scottish Labour College."

The Provisional Committee appointed consisted of the original Committee convening the Conference and an equal number selected from the delegates to the Conference.

The savage sentence of three years imprisonment passed on Maclean on 12th April 1916, had a considerable influence in holding up the work of the College. In the meantime a Plebs League movement began to emerge in Glasgow. Hitherto this movement had been confined to England and found no roots in Scotland, largely because the classes run under the auspices of the B.S.P. and the S.L.P. filled the need.

The initiative towards the formation of groups of " Plebs " came from the S.L.P., which since the beginning of the war had been striving to break away from its former narrow moorings in other directions, and now turned to working class Education. A Glasgow " Plebs League " was formed and classes in Independent Working Class Education were organised mostly with members of the S.L.P. as tutors.

On 16th September, 1917, a Conference was called on the joint appeal of the S.L.P., I.L.P., B.S.P., Herald League and No Conscription Fellowship, two Divisional Councils of the B.S.P. and S.L.P., and sixteen Independent Workers' Groups and Workshop Committees.

Of the three resolutions passed at this Conference the second one was the most important. It was moved by Walton Newbold and said :

" Realising the need for a definite working class Educational platform wherein all sections of the Labour movement can unite and work together for the spread of correct economic knowledge, endorses the aims and methods of the Plebs League and establishes the Glasgow Branch of that organisation."

A big discussion arose on this resolution. John Maclean, who, as we have seen, had been released on 3rd July after serving 14 months and 22 days of his three years sentence, was present as a delegate. If the Scottish Labour movement was not meeting the needs of the moment the fault could not be imputed to Maclean. Indeed, he criticised bitterly those responsible for the neglect of the College whilst he was in prison. In this connection he named his old comrade John F. Armour.

He objected strongly to the formation of the Plebs League, on the ground that the Conference was not taking into account the existing Committee of the Scottish Labour College, and he feared a clash between these two bodies. An amendment was moved to delay forming a branch of the Plebs League for the time being. There voted for the amendment 41, against 49 for the resolution. The support for Maclean was quite substantial, and it was agreed to meet in Conference the Committee of the Scottish Labour College, with a view to a united movement.

By the end of October the new Plebs organisation had organised 20 classes. At the same time the Scottish Labour College were running classes that winter, 1917-18, in Bargeddie, Blantyre, Lesmahagow, Motherwell, Paisley, Kirkintilloch, Greenock, Johnstone, Govan, Leven, Kirkcaldy, Bowhill, Cowdenbeath, Kilsyth and Glasgow, with an aggregate attendance of 1,500 students.

Most of the Labour College classes outside of Glasgow were held on week nights, while the Glasgow class was reserved for Sunday afternoon. Supporting John Maclean as lecturers were James D. MacDougall, J. F. Armour, H. B. Guthrie, R. Nicol and Neil Maclean, subsequently M.P. for Govan.

Following the decision of the " Plebs " conference, negotiations were opened between the West of Scotland Plebs League and the Scottish Labour College and eventually the Plebs League was merged in the Scottish Labour College.

On 16th March, 1918, a Conference was held in the Co-operative Hall, Clarence Street, to consider a draft constitution and curriculum for the proposed College. 271 Branches and 417 delegates attended. The Constitution as drafted by the Committee was passed with very slight amendment (See Appendix). It was at this conference that the first Executive Committee of the Scottish Labour College was formed, with the following as officials : Chairman, John McLure of the I.L.P. ; Secretary, William Leonard, Co-operator (paid) ; Treasurer, F. Rafther ; Tutors, John Maclean (paid) and J. Thomson of

S.L.P. Apart from Leonard and Maclean all the others were unpaid.

Within a month Maclean was once more arrested and his work for the College was interrupted until his release on 3rd December of the same year, just on the eve of the " Coupon " election in 1918. No sooner released than he was active again. On 13th January, 1919, he addressed a packed meeting in Shettleston, Glasgow, on behalf of the Labour College. He was supported at the meeting by the iron-moulder, John McBain, of the S.L.P., an active unpaid lecturer for the College. At this meeting £10 was collected in aid of the College Funds.

In the course of the spring of 1919 a number of district conferences took place. The centres visited were Aberdeen, Arbroath, Dundee, East and West Fife, Edinburgh and Falkirk. The attendances at these meetings was surprisingly good. Some local branches of trade unions agreed to levy their members to nourish the College work in their own districts. Finally, the plans were laid down at a Conference held in the Co-operative Hall, Glasgow, on 24th May, 1919, for the opening of day classes on 1st September of that year. John Maclean and W. McLaine, a member of the B.S.P. from Manchester, were appointed in August as full time tutors. Premises were opened at 96 St. Vincent Street, Glasgow, and nine students attended ; three from the Fife miners, three from the Lanarkshire miners, and three from Glasgow trade union workers.

At the national Conference held in the St. Andrew's Hall, Glasgow, on Saturday, 29th May, 1920, attended by 530 delegates, the Treasurer's report showed that £2,000 had been received during the previous year, and that if the income of all branches and classes were included it would have been something like £2,500.

The success and extent of the Scottish Labour College movement, as the " Glasgow Herald " reported, " surprised the public." The " Herald " took the Labour College to task for its " ill-balanced teaching, based almost entirely on Marx," and went on to boost the " cultural " work of the Workers' Educational Association. It advocated co-operation between the W.E.A. and the College movement. Maclean was extremely critical of such a course. Recalling the experience at Ruskin College, he wrote in "The Vanguard" (July 1920): "That things

will not be all right in the Labour College and that an attempt
to fuse it with the W.E.A. and the Universities, as happened in
the case of Ruskin College, is a justifiable attitude of mind not
only in the light of past events inside the Provisional Committee
(he is here referring to a proposal by McLure to dismiss Maclean
as a Tutor), but also in the light of the significant remarks from
the Labour correspondent in the " Glasgow Herald."

The effect of this note of warning from Maclean was to
produce a resolution from the Provisional Committee, to the
effect " that this, the Provisional Committee of the Scottish
Labour College, repudiate and deny, in the most unqualified
manner, that any arrangement regarding working class education is being entered into with the Workers' Educational
Association ; and that independent working class education on
Marxist lines still continues to be our objective."

To which Maclean replied that he " did not assert that the
Labour College had yet departed from Marxism. The game of
the Government to corrupt working class institutions does not
work out that way, and never will." He was of the opinion
that the Government was working to get him removed, and
then work for an " entente " with the W.E.A.

" Nothing here said," he writes in " The Vanguard," Sept.
1920, " ought to discourage the working class. Spend more
money on the college, send more students to day classes, roll
up to the evening and week-end classes, but all the time keep a
sharp look-out for shoals and rocks. Eternal vigilance is the
price of freedom—and Marxist education."

In raising this note of warning regarding the dangers of
merging the movement for independent working class (Marxist) education with the W.E.A. movement, Maclean showed
shrewdness and sure class instinct. The whole work of the
W.E.A. with its broad " humanist " studies, leads in effect to a
greater dependence of the working class on bourgeois ideas,
culture and social outlook. The aim of working *class* (Marxist)
Education is to free the workers from the baneful grip of
bourgeois ideology ; to educate them to class solidarity, train
revolutionary fighters and to strengthen the working class in
its march towards socialism.

Maclean had the conviction, justly, I think, that the fusion
of the two irreconcilable systems of thought could only serve

to weaken the growth of the advancing class movement of the
workers, on the one hand, and, on the other hand, to strengthen
the persistence of bourgeois ideas and outlook, still deep-rooted
despite the experience of the war, in the trade union and labour
movement.

With the formation of the Communist Party of Great Britain
a new and further development took place in the conceptions
of working class education and its aims. This was the question
of the political education of the members and functionaries of
the Party, and of the political education carried on by the
members and functionaries of the Party among the masses of
the working class outside the Party.

Workers' Education was no longer a matter of broad
"humanist" studies after the manner of the W.E.A. or
"independent" of working class party politics, after the
manner of the Plebs League, then the leading body within the
movement for independent working class education. It was a
vital question, urgent and necessary, to equip the Party, the
advance guard and leader of the whole working class movement, for the revolutionary tasks that stood before it. Henceforth working class education was no longer to be treated as a
separate branch of the working class movement, but as a means
of theoretical equipment, enabling the working class to inter-
pret events and guide it in all its political action and practice.

The educational work of John Maclean was directed towards
the awakening of class-consciousness, an understanding of the
class gulf between the workers and the bourgeoisie ; the preparation of socialist agitators and propagandists, the enlarge-
ment of the movement for the overthrow of capitalism—the
proletarian revolution. His contribution to the realisation of
this aim was great and positive. His weakness lay in the
isolated character of his efforts (particularly in the last years of
the war). How much more extensive and permanent might
have been the results had he laboured, not merely as an ardent
individual, but as a member of a party consecrated to the same
tasks ! He tilled the soil untiringly, and scattered much good
seed ; but only organised activity and collective leadership
could bring all this toil to fruition.

CHAPTER 21

CO-OPERATION

THE many-sided activity of John Maclean included one theatre of action too often neglected by progressive and revolutionary thought—the Co-operative movement. This movement has a long and honourable tradition in Scotland. Indeed, Scotland may be said to be the cradle of the Co-operative movement in this country. As far back as 1769 the weavers of Fenwick, Ayrshire, bought and sold meal for their mutual advantage. In 1777 there was a victualling society started in Govan. In 1800 a similar society existed in Bridgeton, Glasgow. In 1812, a Co-operative Society in Lennoxtown, near Glasgow, was actually paying dividends in proportion to the purchases of its members. One Alexander Campbell, secretary and propagandist lecturer to Robert Owen, claims to have advocated co-operation and dividends on purchases to the miners of Cambuslang. It was from this same Campbell that the Rochdale friends took up the idea and worked it out successfully. They certainly appear to have consulted him when forming their famous Equitable Society in 1843-44.

By 1911 there was scarcely a town or village in Scotland without its local co-operative society. And Pollokshaws was no exception to the rule. Like the great majority of socialists in those days John Maclean was an ardent co-operator. But his interest in co-operation was not that of a mere dividend hunter. As a marxist he was a co-operator by conviction and on principle. The co-operative movement, for Maclean, was a people's challenge to the trusts and monopolies of capitalism—the commissariat of the labour movement, as he was fond of describing it. He took part in the local meetings of the society and attended the district conferences. He took a special interest in the educational work of the society, and became one of their most popular lecturers, visiting local societies all over the country.

Here is what Maclean has to say in the famous paper to which we have already alluded and which he read before the

Renfrewshire Co-operative Conference on 25th November, 1911 :

" The times we live in are so stirring and full of change that it is not impossible to believe we are in the rapids of revolution. Truly, the development in every branch of industrial, commercial, political, social, and intellectual activity is so apparently quick that even the dullest must admit that the old order of society is passing away, to give place to one that with our aid will eradicate for ever the inequalities, the injustices, and the oppression that characterise the present. We have but to think of the increasing thousands of inventions and discoveries that facilitate production ; of the swift spread of the most perfect modes of transit and communication ; of the amazing expansion of capitalism through the export of capital from developed to undeveloped countries ; of the unprecedented grabbing of occupied lands for the extension of trade and of empires ; of the sudden arrival of mammoth trusts controlling colossal masses of capital and slaves ; of the tremendous uprise of the masses in the Co-operative, the trade union, and the socialist movements, to find a growing expression in productive and distributive activity, economic revolt, and political agitation ; of the modern political upheavals, starting six years ago in Russia and passing in rapid succession through Turkey, Persia, Portugal, and Mexico, to find a momentary culmination in China, in what may ripen into the most magnificent and dramatic transformation ever witnessed by man—I say, we have but to think of all this to catch but the faintest outline of a world change that is so truly indicative of the triumph of knowledge and its application over the chaos of the past, and of the ultimate ascendency of the organised masses over the forces and the resources of the world. These are but a few of the outward and visible signs of the evolution of capitalism—an evolution so fraught with impending dangers to the Co-operative movement that it is our imperative duty to investigate from all possible standpoints the nature and the extent of these dangers, and thus prepare to adopt such new methods and agencies as will enable us to survive under the new commercial conditions so rapidly rising above the economic horizon."

Maclean then takes a rapid glance back in history, treats of the industrial revolution in the eighteenth century, the birth of the factory system, the rise of the capitalist class and the coming of the Rochdale system of Co-operation. He passes on to the questions of competition between traders, advancing wages and dropping prices. The fall of prices from 1876 to 1896 certainly had an effect on the people, who, under such favourable conditions, were less inclined to leave retailers for whom they personally had a liking. Certain it is that the rivals both flourished during that period if the number of shops be any index of development, for between 1875 and 1895 the number of shops rose from 295,000 to 408,850—an increase of almost thirty-nine per cent. in twenty-two years. Under the circumstances, it was impossible for private traders to build up such an efficient organisation as could crush out the co-operative stripling. When they did get alarmed it was too late ; co-operation had struck its roots too deep and spread its branches too wide."

Speaking of the rise of the multiple shop he says : " In 1896, whilst this new departure was in its infancy, a change had also manifested itself in the price of commodities. From the 'seventies till the 'nineties prices had steadily fallen, as already indicated, but by 1896 the tide turned and from that date till this prices have steadily risen, till at present they are from fifteen to twenty per cent. higher. That they will still continue to rise is well known ; how long, is only known to the gods. At first the rise was not felt by the working class because from 1895 to 1900, a period of expanding trade, wages rose. But since 1900 prices have gone up ten per cent. whilst wages have dropped over £92,000 per week and unemployment has become more prevalent. This means that the workers' purchasing power within the first decade of this century has considerably declined, a situation accentuated by a rise in rents and rates of forty per cent. in many cases. And, as we know, this year of grace (1911) is experiencing exorbitant prices for sugar, eggs, butter, cheese and other commodities, with little or no relaxation in those of the remainder."

Examining the question of rising prices, he maintains that these will continue to rise, one of the causes being the rapidly growing output of gold from the year 1890 to 1910, citing

statistics to prove it. The workers' position in these circumstances, he contends, is bound to grow worse. As to the
awakening of the trade unions and the formation of associations such as the Transport Workers' Federation, he is not so
sanguine that they will be able to counteract the rise by forcing
up wages. This did not mean that there should be no efforts
made.

" I can claim some credit," he says, " since January for
forcing on the notice of socialists and trade unionists alike the
extent of price-rising and the need for higher wages." A statement which illustrates the kind of work he was doing in his
public meetings and study classes. Yet he noted that with all
the striking and agitating that summer the net increases in
wages had fallen far short of the £92,000 lost since the century
began. Wages, he contended, would recede again when trade
turned bad, " unless powerful industrial unions have been
established ready at a moment's notice to pursue the ' down
tools ' policy.

" I hold that one result of the intensified poverty of the
people, due mainly to rising prices, has been the crushing of the
private traders, whose customers have either come to our
societies or gone to the multiple shops. This is obvious when
we know that from 1900 to 1906 only 21,000 shops were added
to the former number, an average of 3,000 per annum, compared with the average of nearly 6,000 for the last twenty-five
years of the nineteenth century. As it is estimated that over
70,000 shops are owned by multiple companies, and that many
new shops have been added by our societies this century, we
may safely conclude that there has been a decided shrinkage
in shops owned by private traders. When we reckon that the
stress of the times has forced many poor people into " wee"
shops to supplement other sources of income, and that the
business of many old established firms is rapidly dwindling to
the zero point, we begin to comprehend the transformation
taking place. The keener struggle to make ends meet has
submerged the old sentiment binding the housewife to the
retailer. As we have seen, with the sentiment is going the
retailer too."

Quoting statistics Maclean shows that members have been
attracted to the co-operative movement despite the rise in

co-operative prices, goes on to give evidence of the growth of the multiple system, with disastrous consequences to private retailers, but also with potential danger to the Co-operative movement, and urges upon the co-operators not to sit back and be content with a little progress but to take up the challenge.

" For our movement to let the potential enemy grow more rapidly than itself is, I repeat, to court utter disaster. Hence the need for taking steps calculated to spread our system to the limits of the population, if possible." . . . " I, for one, feel triumphantly hopeful as I recognise that the coming conflict between the capitalist trusts and co-operation will be but another aspect of the great class war that inevitably must lead to the victory of the workers by the overthrow of capitalist predominance. That co-operation is going to play a great historic part in the ultimate transformation of society I am convinced, or it would have little of my time."

Here follows a concrete analysis of the methods of the monopolists in controlling the supply and prices of raw materials, the boycott of the co-operative societies, and Maclean's views as to what should be done.

" What should we do to meet all possible types of opposition ? So far as adulteration is concerned we should help on any movement compelling the Government to intervene on behalf of innocent purchasers and of the health of the community. Suffice for that. Next, I strongly hold that the depreciation of plant and property should be increased at the expense of a reduced dividend. Some of us years ago howled at the Wholesale on the trust question, and the outcome was increased depreciation. Since then managers and society directors have demanded a reduction of this rate of depreciation so as to get a bigger dividend from the Wholesale. These poor souls are prepared to sacrifice anyone and anything to keep up a dividend often misjudged by present competition. *I would hang one or two as a warning to the others !* The Scottish Wholesale gives 8d. per £ dividend whereas the English Wholesale gives only 4d. I would advise the Scottish directors to gradually reduce theirs to 4d. as well, and use the difference to hasten depreciation. They should also clear out surplus capital by reducing their various rates of interest and thus set the example to retail societies. These latter must likewise

L

reduce the rate of interest and increase the rate of depreciation, while yet the day remaineth. Over and above, the reserve funds should be more speedily inflated so that ultimately interest-bearing capital may be dispensed with. The ideal is thus property absolutely free of charges and a further capital free of interest, able to be used at any moment for extension purposes or making good any losses incurred by selling under cost price. And yet all this could not save separate societies when facing a national trust as the latter is a higher form of co-operation than ours. We must, in consequence, also evolve such a higher form by the ultimate establishment of a national co-operative society. None comprehend the dangers to democracy in such a proposal more clearly than I do, but I am confident that the suggested co-operation of co-operative organisations could ultimately be founded on a democratic basis.

" I am out, then, for the abolition of interest and dividend, with free capital and a national society as the best basic conditions in the struggle. I am out for high wages and short hours to all workers as long as capitalism lasts, and, therefore, if we are going to do justice to our servants we must have a fusion of two trade unions and the growth of a solidified union for the whole distributive trade linked up with the Transport Workers' Federation. By such means will we prevent the enemy beating us through sweated labour. Lastly, we will have to bring our methods up to date. A national society could do this better than individual ones, and hence I am confident that when we reach this stage of our development we will not be defeated by the enemy carrying on trade at a less expense.

" Bear in mind I have no fear of the future. The working class is going to win by the establishment of socialism even were co-operation to go under. But the working class cannot afford to let this great popular movement sink under the opposition of the class that, having performed its work in history, must inevitably yield supremacy to ours, the last class to attain freedom. In my eyes, just as trade unionism is playing its part, so also must co-operation in the great human impulse towards that time when, the world-wide co-operative commonwealth having been established, man for the first time shall rise dictator over the forces and resources of nature, and ensured through life of the material, mental, and moral requisites of a grand and noble existence, shall also for the first time cease from robbery and cease from conflict."

It may be seen from the content of this paper, and from his article on "Labour's Commissariat Department," that Maclean had sound ideas with regard to the role of the co-operative movement in the class struggle. He did not take the traditional view of labour people and socialists that the co-operative movement was the third form of the labour movement, leading an independent existence with its own ideology and politically neutral in the class struggle. He fought against the bourgeois influences in the management and direction of co-operative affairs ; against the pursuit of interest and dividends as an end in itself. He rightly demanded that the co-operatives assist the working class in its battles against high prices and the exploitation of the public generally by the multiple stores through monopoly prices.

When he likened the co-operative movement to " Labour's Commissariat Department," he had in mind not merely the provision of food and victuals by a non-capitalist, non-profiteering institution. To Maclean the co-operative movement must be an integral part of the working class movement, assisting the workers in strikes and lockouts to defeat the starvation weapon so often used by the capitalists ; helping the unemployed during periods of crisis, and preparing to supply the people with all the necessary foodstuffs in the event of revolution.

The experience of the co-operative organisation in Russia during the revolution showed how just was Maclean's fight against the bourgeois ideas that largely dominate the administration and management of co-operative societies in a capitalist country. The Russian workers had to face resistance and all manner of obstructions from reactionary leaders of the co-operatives in Russia. It was necessary to thoroughly overhaul the Russian co-operatives, to clean out all the bourgeois elements, before the societies could begin to assume their true social function as a commissariat department of the Workers' Socialist Republic.

Maclean's criticism of the administration of the co-operative movement for not energetically fighting the trusts and multiple stores, or for merely imitating the forms of the capitalist concerns was in the right direction. The co-operative societies, as at present constituted and led, assume too much the character of a joint-stock company. The enormous funds of the co-operatives are locked up in municipal and government stocks as " safe investments " for their shareholders. The co-operatives are thus integrated with the bourgeois state.

The bourgeois outlook of the co-operative society is not confined to economic affairs. It seeks to protect its special interests by a co-operative political party independent even of the Labour Party, a denial of the conception of the co-operatives as an integral part of the labour and socialist movement. The Co-operative Party insists upon its own private interests as the concern of the co-operators alone, and often in antagonism to the Labour Party. The keen critical mind of Maclean was alive to these influences. At the same time, knowing the membership of the co-operative societies to be overwhelmingly proletarian, he addressed himself vigorously to that membership, confident of its ability to overcome these influences and give the movement a positive and anti-capitalist character.

It is as a pioneer of this conscious revolutionary conception of the role of co-operation that he will be remembered and appreciated by co-operators of the future.

CONCLUSION

THE twenty-one years that marked the political life of John Maclean correspond to a well defined period of growth in the working class movement of Scotland. The drift away from liberal-labourism towards a political party independent of the two old parties, Liberals and Tories, begun in the previous decade, had assumed definite shape with the formation of the Labour Representation Committee in 1900. It was crystallised with the conversion of the latter into the Labour Party in 1906, and culminated in the advent of the first labour government in January 1924, one month after the death of Maclean.

This period may be represented as an ascending curve in working class history, having clearly defined forms of political activity, peculiar to the epoch. It had all the marks of youth, an intense activity and vigour in propaganda carried out with a remarkable zeal, enthusiasm and faith in the certain victory of the working class and socialism.

The period was also marked by a wave of intellectual questioning in the realm of politics, economics, history, philosophy, sociology and the physical sciences. In the homes of most militant and serious minded workers a modest library was to be found containing standard works on some or all of these subjects. Cheap reprints of the great thinkers of the nineteenth century found a wide public and a ready sale. A great deal of serious reading and healthy discussion went on. Side by side with general propaganda meetings, lectures on highly theoretical problems attracted large audiences. So great was the ferment of thought that large numbers of bourgeois intellectuals, journalists and writers of all creeds and parties were brought into action to refute and confound the revolutionary doctrines and theories of socialism, in particular, the theories of Marx and Engels. It was in such a milieu that the educational work of John Maclean was undertaken.

It was inevitable in such circumstances that differences should exist between the militants of the trade unions, the labour and socialist groups. The pure and simple trade unionists were sceptical of the ideas of socialism. The Independent Labour Party, the largest and most influential section of the advancing labour movement drew its inspiration from the broad humanitarianism of Keir Hardie, and from the popular writings of Robert Blatchford (" Merrie England," " Britain for the British "). The Marxists, on the other hand, concentrated on explaining the relations between wage-labour and capital and the inevitability of the class struggle, and propounding the teachings of scientific socialism with its corrollary, the social revolution. But running through all these differences like a red thread, agreement was general, with the exception of a small group here and there, on the common desire to see a strong political party of the working class that would one day oust the two parties of capitalism, and take over the government of the country.

Maclean, as we have seen, held firmly to this general conception of the period. Being a revolutionary socialist did not prevent him from participating in the broader movement of the Labour Party. It was his conviction that the working class would come to socialism through struggle and out of their own experience. In this respect he comes nearest of all his contemporaries to the injunction of Marx, Engels and Lenin. Like these great teachers he was aware of the corrupting influence of the bourgeoisie upon the workers' movement, and did not fear to criticise those reactionary leaders who refused to wage the class struggle and capitulated to capitalism. Nor did he fear to criticise openly the leaders of the co-operative movement.

When the first imperialist world war took place he attacked the labour leaders for their chauvinism and denounced the Glasgow labour leaders who were in favour of a " political truce " for the duration of the war. He supported every measure of direct action adopted by the trade union workers, appealing to the leaders to take the lead, and criticising them when they failed. In the circumstances of the period his life is a complete example of self-sacrifice and subordination of personal interests to the larger interests of the working class and socialism, a contrast to the hesitation, vacillation and opportunism of the great majority of his contemporaries.

His approach to the question of the war was the approach of the Marxist. The war was the outcome of imperialist rivalry and contradictions between contending capitalist groups. The difficulties of the bourgeois class provided opportunities for the working class. He would have the working class utilise these opportunities. The defence of economic interests ought not to be limited to defensive action. He would take the offensive ; organise it for the general strike, and through that to the proletarian revolution.

It was not surprising that he got little response from the influential leaders, official and unofficial. The majority of trade union leaders would not go beyond purely economic aims. The political leaders, municipal councillors, and members of the Independent Labour Party, though flirting with socialism, merely sought to canalise the worker's unrest and revolt into parliamentary channels. To this Maclean would not have been opposed, for he saw no contradiction between industrial and parliamentary action. His challenge was to their faith in " gradualism," to their refusal to fulfil the socialist principle of class struggle and to give revolutionary class leadership, precisely in conditions favourable to the working class.

When in 1922 the Labour Party did achieve considerable successes at the polls no one better appreciated the results than Maclean. For him it was an advance of the working class movement towards the ultimate conquest of political power. He understood the limitations of the parliamentary institutions. He did not expect the parliamentary labour group to bring socialism into being overnight. But he did expect, and justly so in the light of the propaganda work of a whole generation, that they, especially the Scottish members, would adopt a challenging attitude to all vested interests and speak fearlessly in the name of socialism and the working class that sent them to " Westminster ; " that they would translate the hopes and expectations of the last twenty years of socialist propaganda into deeds.

Maclean had ever been the mortal enemy of bourgeois respectability and constitutional formality. This we have seen in his earliest activities on behalf of the unemployed and in his struggles during the war and after the war. Catching the " atmosphere of the House," being flattered and fawned upon, posing and play-acting in face of the class enemy was detestable to Maclean. And when he suggested that the Scottish Labour members would have been better employed had they stayed at home instead of going to Westminster, he was expressing more than the influence of the Irish Republicans upon him, great as this was in his latter days ; he was expressing his inner conviction as to the influence of bourgeois ideas on the Labour members. In this respect, the Labour Government of 1924, and more so that of 1928, showed he was not far wrong.

The Irish Republican movement, as we have seen, had a great influence on Maclean. He would adopt the same methods for Scotland. What he failed to see, or take into sufficient consideration, was the peculiar features and background of the Irish Republican movement, in particular that the Irish movement was the culmination of years of political repression ; of trial and experience in the British parliamentary system. Preceding the boycott of the British House of Commons a whole movement had been going on for years in the spirit of nationalism, including the revival of the Irish language, literature, drama, and the preparation of physical resistance to the rule of the alien English. To adopt the methods of the Irish Republicans, to call upon the Scottish Labour members to boycott Westminster and to set up a Scottish council or parliament was unreal in the circumstances when no such traditions or condition existed ; the more so since none of the Labour members ever subscribed to revolutionary action.

John Maclean had most of the higher qualities that make for political leadership. He combined a high standard of general education with a wide knowledge of Marxism. Though cautious in temperament, he was a man of action, and endowed with great moral courage. Thickset and physically strong, he was fearless in face of danger, and tenacious in purpose to the point of fanaticism. The injustices of the industrial system awoke in his sympathetic nature a burning desire to seek redress. No one ever appealed to Maclean for assistance in vain. He was no snob, and went direct to the source of a grievance regardless of persons or institutions. He remained to the last a man of socialist convictions and principle.

But for political leadership something more is needed besides personal qualities. A *party* is necessary, embodying collective experience and collective criticism of mistakes and successes. The B.S.P., to which Maclean belonged, was weak in numbers and *personnel* in Scotland. During the war, as Maclean frankly acknowledged at a social gathering of his party friends, the question of party had been neglected and subordinated to mass action. And since he had no powerful trade union connections, his activities became individualistic and without collective guidance. When, finally, the question of a new type of party was raised, particularly following the Russian Revolution, he was unable to rise above personal antipathies and a limited national outlook. He came under the influence of the popular mass demonstrations. He saw the revolution coming out of spontaneous mass movement and the general strike. He did not seem to realise that a political general strike if successful would necessarily develop into insurrection, that, as Marx insisted, " insurrection is an art quite as much as war or any other," and that for that a centralised political party was necessary.

Had his health remained robust, he might well have learned (as many others of us did) from the experience of the revolutionary period following the war and have clarified his ideas in the course of international discussion. But, as we have seen, he had paid a heavy price in physical strength.

It would be grossly unfair to condemn John Maclean for the weaknesses he exhibited, following his prison experiences. Life in our prisons is no joke, least of all in penal servitude. It is a serious trial for the toughest of men. But its effects on the individual prisoner are largely determined by his attitude towards it. Some men of sensitive nature can pass through and come out unscathed, where men of sterner stuff are broken. Conversely, some impressionable natures will go all to pieces where a little conscious firmness would have saved them. The best defence for the political prisoner is to make up his mind from the day of entry to treat the experience as being " all in the day's work." Within the measure of possibilities (possibilities which he has the duty to explore and create), he should establish contacts with other political prisoners, and maintain the liveliest connections with the organised movement outside. Above all to have the firm determination to maintain the high morale worthy of the cause he serves ; to keep fit so that on release he may be able to immediately take up his work again. But in the absence of such considerations the rebel, combative nature of John Maclean would not be restrained, and he paid the penalty. His health seriously impaired, his soul embittered with hatred for the authorities who unquestionably set out to destroy him and through him strike at the workers' movement, it was not surprising he was unable to bring to bear upon the new tasks the same measure of sound judgment that characterised him in the pre-war years.

With a few personal admirers he did indeed attempt to set up a party, but it was no longer a party in line with the new international movement to which in spirit he really belonged. It was to be a purely Scottish Workers' Republican Party. In point of fact a few camp followers sought to continue after his death the work of building such a party, but without success.

Those weaknesses apart, by his devotion, heroism and disinterested loyalty to the cause of the working class movement, John Maclean will for ever be revered as a true son of the Scottish people—and a dauntless fighter for freedom.

APPENDIX I.

CONSTITUTION

NAME—The Scottish Labour College.

OBJECT—The training of men and women in such subjects and on such lines as shall equip them for Trade Union and Political activities in the interest of the working class.

ORGANISATION

CONTROL—The College shall be governed by an Executive Committee composed of a President, Secretary, Treasurer, and nine others.

They shall be elected at a Biennial Conference.

They shall carry out the instructions of the Biennial Conference and shall act as a Board of Supervision.

They shall have powers to appoint and dismiss all members of the Staff, and to fix fees or salaries—the salaries fixed to be the same for each member of the staff, whether Principal or Assistant.

They shall elect out of their number Three Trustees, in whose names, along with that of the Treasurer, all money shall be deposited. No money shall be drawn from the Bank except on order signed by any two of the Trustees and the Treasurer.

The Biennial Conference shall be composed of Delegates from each Society, District Council, or Branch of working class organisation subscribing towards the upkeep of the College.

Sources of income :

1. Grants from Trade Unions on the basis of 3d. per member per annum.
2. Donations from Co-operative, Socialist and Labour Societies.

3. Fees from Day Students, £5 per term of three months. Subscribing Societies can send a student for every £2 per annum subscribed at a fee of £3 per term of three months.

NOTE.—Nos. 1 and 2 are only suggestions. Each organisation will of course contribute in accordance with its Constitution and Rules. Trade Unions by grants, donations and levies, etc.; Co-operative Societies by Educational Grants, and Labour and Socialist Organisations have methods, peculiar to themselves, of raising money for projects with which they are in sympathy.

District Committees organising Classes under the auspices of the College will also assist, and there is a vast field for sympathisers through works subscriptions. No College or University is supported by the fees it charges, still less will it be the case of a Labour College. The Labour College must be subsidised by Organised Labour.

CURRICULUM

There shall be three terms per annum, each of three months duration, viz. : October till December, January till March, April till June.

The subjects taught shall include :

1. Economics.
2. General and Industrial History.
3. History, Structure, and Problems of Trade Unionism.
4. History, Structure, and Problems of Co-operation.
5. Laws affecting Labour.
6. Political Science.
7. Arithmetic, Algebra and Statistics.
8. English Literature, Composition and Public Speaking.
9. Business methods applied to Trade Unions and Labour Organisations, including Book-keeping and Typewriting.

APPENDIX II.

John Maclean's speech from the dock given in Edinburgh, Thursday, May 9th, 1918.

It has been said that they cannot fathom my motive. For the full period of my active life I have been a teacher of Economics to the working classes, and my contention has always been that Capitalism is rotten to its foundations, and must give place to a new society. I had a lecture, the principal heading of which was " Thou shalt not steal ; thou shalt not kill," and I pointed out that as a consequence of the robbery that goes on in all civilised countries to-day, our respective countries have had to keep armies, and that inevitably our armies must clash together. On that and on other grounds, I consider Capitalism the most infamous, bloody and evil system that mankind has ever witnessed. My language is regarded as extravagant language, but the events of the past four years have proved my contention.

THE CLASS WAR

He (the Lord Advocate) accused me of my motives. My motives are clean. My motives are genuine. If my motives were not clean and genuine, would I have made my statements while these short-hand reporters were present ? I am out for the benefit of society, not for any individual human being, but I realise this that Justice and Freedom can only be obtained when Society is placed on a sound economic basis. That sound economic basis is wanting to-day, and hence the bloodshed we are having. I have not tried to get young men particularly. The young men have come to my meetings as well as the old men. I know quite well that in the reconstruction of Society, the class interests of those who are on top will resist the change, and the only factor in Society that can make for a clean sweep in Society is the working class. Hence the Class War. The whole history of Society has proved that Society moves forward as a consequence of an under class overcoming the resistance of a class on top of them. So much for that.

I also wish to point out to you this, that when the late King Edward the Seventh died, I took as the subject of one of my lectures " Edward the Peacemaker." I pointed out at the time that his " entente cordiale " with France and his alliance with Russia were for the purpose of encircling Germany as a result of the coming friction between Germany and this country because of commercial rivalry. I then denounced that title " Edward the Peacemaker," and said that it should be " Edward the War-maker." The events which have ensued prove my contention right up to the hilt. I am only proceeding along the lines upon which I have proceeded for many years. I have pointed out at my Economic classes that, owing to the surplus created by the workers, it was necessary to create a market outside this country, because of the inability of the workers to purchase the wealth they create. You must have markets abroad, and in order to have these markets you must have empire. I have also pointed out that the capitalist development of Germany since the Franco-Prussian War has forced upon that country

the necessity for empire as well as this country, and in its search for
empire there must be a clash between these two countries. I have been
teaching that and what I have taught is coming perfectly true.

I wish no harm to any human being, but I, as one man, am going to
exercise my freedom of speech. No human being on the face of the
earth, no government is going to take from me my right to speak, my
right to protest against wrong, my right to do everything that is for the
benefit of mankind. *I am not here, then, as the accused ; I am here as the
accuser of Capitalism dripping with blood from head to foot.*

In connection with the " ca' canny " question at Parkhead Forge,
I wish to take up some of the particular points first of all before I deal
with the revolution. It is quite evident that it was in connection with a
report in the " Forward " that reference was made to David Kirkwood.
It was there reported that Kirkwood had made a record output. Now
David Kirkwood, representing the Parkhead Forge workers, at the end
of 1915, when the dilution of labour began, put forward a printed
statement for the benefit of Mr. Lloyd George and his colleagues, the
first sentence of which, in big type, was—" What you wish is greater
output." He said that the Parkhead Forge workers were then prepared
to give a greater output and accept dilution if they, the workers, had
some control over the conditions under which the greater output would
accrue. That was his contention. Since he was got into position he
seems to have boasted that he has got a record output. The question
was put to me. Was this consistent with the position and with the
attitude of the working class ? I said it was not consistent with the
attitude and the position of the working class, that his business was to
get back right down to the normal, to " ca' canny " so far as the
general output was concerned.

THE CA' CANNY POLICY

The country has been exploited by the Capitalists in every sphere, to
get the toilers to work harder to bring victory. I said at the commencement of the war that while this was being done, and while assurances
were being given that at the end of the war the people would get back
to normal, I said that circumstances would make such a return impossible. Now I have ample evidence to support that belief ; I have used
it at my meetings at Weir's of Cathcart—that they were asking the
workers to toil harder, not only during the war, but after the war they
wish them to work harder and harder, because there is going to be " the
war after the war," the economic war which brought on this war. You
see, therefore, the workers are brought into a position where they are
speeded up, and they are never allowed to go back again. They are
speeded up again and again. What is the position of the worker ? This
country is not a free country. The worker is deprived of land or access
to the land ; he is deprived of workshops or access to the materials and
tools of production ; the worker has only one thing to do in the market,
and that is to sell his labour power. The Capitalist purchases that
labour power, and when he gets the worker inside the workshop, his
business is to extract as much of that labour power out of him as
possible. On the other hand, when it comes to wages, then the employer

applies the principle of " ca' canny." " Ca' canny " is quite justifiable when it comes to the employer giving wages to the workers, and we have seen it since the commencement of the war. Prices rose right away from the commencement of the war while the workers' wages were kept at the old normal. Their wages were kept low. The purchasing power of the workers' wages was therefore diminished. They were therefore robbed to that extent. At the same time the workers were asked in the name of the country to work harder, " but," said the employers, " we will not give you any more money, although the money you are getting is purchasing less in the way of food, etc." That is the position.

The employers are changing their opinions now as a result of experience, but in the past they considered it in their economic interest to pay as low a wage as possible. On the other hand the position of the workers is to give as little of their energy as they possibly can and to demand the highest wage possible. If it is right for the employer to get the maximum of energy and pay the minimum of wage, then it is equally right for the worker to give the minimum of his energy and demand the maximum of wage.

What is right for the one is equally right for the other, although the interests of the two classes are diametrically opposed. That is the position, and in view of the fact that many of the workers have over-worked themselves and have had to lie off through overstrain, and considering the treatment they get when thrown on the scrap-heap—kicked out like dogs when they are no longer useful—they are compelled to look after their own welfare. The worker has therefore in the past adopted the policy of " ca' canny," and I have in the interests of the working class advocated the policy of "ca' canny," not because I am against the war, but, knowing that after the war the worker will have the new conditions imposed upon him, I hold still to the principle of " ca' canny." I accede to that.

So far as Parkhead Forge is concerned I also pointed out that none of the great big guns had been made for some time prior to the great offensive. When the offensive came, Gough, the friend of Sir Edward Carson, the man who before the war was going to cut down the Irishmen, retreated and lost so many guns, and then the Glasgow workers had to give over their Easter holiday in order to make those guns. We have, therefore, Beardmore and others responsible for shortage of certain material, and we know from further disclosures that millions of shells have been useless, and perhaps that has been due to the fact of over-speeding, so that even over-speeding may do nothing for the advancement of the war. Furthermore, if big reserves of material are going to be built up, and the Germans are to be allowed to get them, that is going to be to the advantage of the Germans, and not to the advantage of the British.

" DOWN TOOLS " AND FOOD

With regard to the next point, " down tools," so far as Glasgow is concerned, I do not think I told the workers to " down tools." I am of the opinion that I said—" Now that you are determined to " down tools," it is of no use standing idle ; you must do something for your-selves." As a matter of fact my statement was based on a resolution that had been passed by the A.S.E. in the Clyde area, the official Engineers' Committee. It met and it determined to down tools against the introduction of the Man Power Bill.

At the same time that was supplemented by unofficial effort at Geddes' meeting in the City Hall. There a resolution was put up by the workers and carried virtually unanimously, that if the Man Power Bill was put into operation, the Clyde district workers would " down tools." It was unnecessary for me, therefore, in light of these official and unofficial statements, to urge the " down tools " policy.

As a matter of fact, we were told that the Government had dismissed many munition girls just immediately prior to the great offensive, so that if the workers are guilty of stoppage of output of munitions, the Government is likewise responsible in the dismissal of those thousands of girls.

Now then, food and farms. I pointed out to the workers that what was necessary if they stopped work was the getting of food. There had been a shortage ; the Government had held up the supplies, for several reasons probably—perhaps to get this rationing passed, in order to have a tight hold on food, and also lest the people get out of hand in reference to this Man Power Bill. I knew that there was plenty of food in stores in Glasgow, and that the farmers had food stored up in their farms. · The farmers have used the war in order to make huge profits for themselves, and then the Government assisted them in connection with the potato regulations ; and latterly, at the end of last year the Corn Production Act was passed, not in the interests of the farm labourers, but in the interests of the farmers.

When the demand for more food production was made, the farmers said they would do their best, and the Government refused to give the farm labourers a minimum wage of 25s. to 30s. a week—25s. at that time being equivalent to 10s. in normal times. The farmers were going to get extra as a consequence of the Corn Production Act. I therefore pointed out that if the workers went to the farmers and did not get the the food stored up in the farms, they should burn the farms. We as Socialists have no interest in destroying any property. We want property to be kept because we want that property to be used for housing accommodation or other reasons, but I specially emphasised about the farmers for the purpose of drawing attention to this particular point.

In the same way, when it came to a question of seizing the Press, I suggested that when the " Daily Record " was seized, the plant should be broken up. I did not say that in connection with the " Glasgow Herald." I said so in connection with the " Record," not that it is a good thing to break up printing plant, but in order to draw attention to the Harmsworth family and to the Rothermeres and so on, and their vile press, which seems to be an index of the culture of Britain. I mention that particularly here, that I said the " Record " plant should be broken up, in order to emphasise the disgust of the organised workers with regard to that particular family or newspapers.

The Women and Children

So far as Ireland and America are concerned, that was mentioned particularly for the purpose of getting food from the St. Lawrence, food from the United States, and food from the Argentine. What was needed was food in order to hold our own, for, as the " Glasgow Herald " pointed out, when the Bolsheviks first came into power, Britain was withholding food from Russia, in the expectation that frost and famine would overthrow the Bolsheviks. That is to say, they were anxious to murder women and children inside Russia, as well as men. The suggestion I made was in order to draw the attention of the workers to the need of having plenty of food stuffs to keep them going.

So far as the Government's responsibitliy for the murder of women and children is concerned, the reason for my statement is perfectly obvious. They have been accusing the Germans of killing women and children in this country. Perfectly true. Of course bombs dropped in Germany have not killed women and children, marvellous to say ! But that apart ; we had the Government getting hold of the food supplies immediately prior to, and immediately after the New Year, and creating a shortage. The Government was therefore responsible for the queues.

Women were standing in queues in the cold, and women had died of what they had contracted during their standing in the queues. The women had died therefore in consequence of the action of the Government, and I threw the responsibility upon the Government—and I do so still.

We know that women and children—human material—have been used up inside the factories, and the housing of the working class in this country has been so bad, and is so bad to-day, that the women and children of the working class die in greater proportion than the women and children of the better-to-do classes. I have always pointed out that the death rate among the working classes has always exceeded that in the better-to-do districts.

I also pointed out that the British Government had sent Russian subjects back to Russia to fight, and had given their wives 12s. 6d. per week and 2s. 6d. for each child. Now, when I was functioning as Russian Consul, two deputations of Russian women came to me and they told me sorrowful tales of depression, disease and death in consequence of the fact that they had received 12s. 6d. per week and 2s. 6d. for each child. I wrote to the Secretary for Scotland in regard to that, and I received no reply. The children ought not to suffer because their fathers have been taken, but those children have suffered. There is not a Lithuanian family in the West of Scotland but has trouble to-day as a consequence of the starving of these people. These women and children of the Russian community have died as a consequence of the meagre supplies given to them by the British Government, and I seize this opportunity for the purpose of making my statement public, in connection with these women, in the hope that the public in general will press the Government to see that these women and children are attended to at least on the same scale as the wives and dependents of British soldiers.

M

AMERICAN " INDEPENDENCE "

With regard to the Yankees, I said, and I say to-day, that the Yankees are out for themselves. The British Press—the British Capitalist Press—sneered and jeered at the Americans before the Americans came in, and pointed out how the Americans were making piles of profit out of the war, but were not participating in this fight for so-called freedom. Those insults were offered to America, and when Mr. Woodrow Wilson said that America was too proud to fight, then that was used venomously. Therefore, if I erred, I erred on the same side as the capitalist class of this country. I made the statement on American authority, not off my own bat. My authority is Professor Roland G. Usher, Professor of History at Washington University. I think his statement in " Pan-Americanism " is one of the finest, showing the moves throughout the world leading up to this war, and Usher has his bias in favour of Britain.

What I wish to particularly refer to are his two books, " Pan-Germanism " and " The Challenge of the Future." In " Pan-Germanism " he surveys North and South and Central America. He takes the Atlantic first, and explains what will be the consequence of the war as regards South and Central America whichever side wins, and then he takes the Pacific. He works it out from a material and economic point of view, his purpose being to get Central and South America to work in with the United States. In his later book he modifies that position—that is to say, in " The Challenge of the Future." He points out that America is still to-day economically dependent, that is to say, she has got to pay interest to financiers in France, in Britain, and therefore America cannot afford to carry out the bold schemes referred to in his book " Pan-Americanism."

I may now state that to-day the business men of this country know perfectly well that the Yankees are boasting of their independence. Therefore when you see references to American independence, that means that she no longer needs to pay interest to investors from outside, and that her policy will be modified in consequence of that new phase. This gentleman points out that as a consequence of American dependence she must say which side she will take. This book was printed prior to America entering the war. Woodrow Wilson's policy works in admirably with the suggestions in that book of Professor Usher, " The Challenge of the Future."

ALLIES AND THE BOLSHEVIKS

We know quite well, too, that the United States of America prevented Japan in 1915 getting economic and political control over North China. Twenty-one articles were imposed on China after the Japs had released their grip of the Germans there. America, alive to her own interests, getting to know of these 21 points, forced Japan to withdraw. America was there working in her own interests.

Japan has been, I think, incited to land at Vladivostock in consequence of the Russian Revolution, and in order to crush the Bolsheviks. The allies on both sides are united to crush the Bolsheviks. America did not take that course. America, early on, began to back up the Bolsheviks because America was afraid that, if Japan got half Siberian Russia, that would give her a strategic control of Siberia, and it would mean a closed door to American contact across the Pacific with Russia proper. America therefore has been looking to her own interests, and for that reason I contend that the Yankees, who have been the worshippers of the mighty dollar, are looking after their own interests in the present war ; and, as to the great boast they have been making about what they are going to do, and their inadequate returns—that, I think, shows that America has not been over-anxious to plunge right away into this war and made all the sacrifices she has said. I know, of course, that America has had her own troubles at home, racial troubles, and also troubles with the workers. Numerous strikes have taken place in America since the commencement of the war, not only in consequence of the war, but also in connection with the economic position.

Some British Atrocities

Now then, I come to the doctors. The doctors I referred to were the prison doctors. When I was in Peterhead it was plain sailing until the middle of December, and then the trouble began. I was fevered up, and being able to combat that, I was then chilled down. Two men came to see me at the end of December, a prominent lecturer in this country, and Mr. Sutherland, M.P., and to them I protested that my food was being drugged. I said that there was alcohol in the food lowering my temperature. I know that potassium bromide is given to people in order to lower their temperature. It may have been potassium bromide that was used in order to lower my temperature. I was aware of what was taking place in Peterhead from hints and statements by other prisoners there ; that from January to March, the so-called winter period, the doctor is busy getting the people into the hospital, there breaking up their organs and their systems.

I call that period the eye-squinting period, because the treatment then given puts the eyes out of view. Through numerous expedients I was able to hold my own. I saw these men round about me in a horrible plight. I have stated in public since that I would rather be immediately put to death than condemned to a life sentence in Peterhead. Attacks were made upon the organs of these men and also upon their nervous systems, and we know from the conscientious objectors that the Government have taken their percentage of these men—some have died, some have committed suicide, others have been knocked off their heads, and in this way got into asylums. The very same process has gone on there. Mrs. Hobhouse has done a good service to mankind in registering the facts. but, unfortunately for Mrs. Hobhouse, she does not know how the result has been obtained. I experienced part of the process, and I wish to emphasise the fact that this callous and cold system of destroying people is going on inside prisons now.

Whatever is done to me now, I give notice that I take no food inside your prisons, absolutely no food ; because of the treatment that was meted out to me. If food is forced upon me, and if I am forcibly fed, then my friends have got to bear in mind that if any evil happens to me,

I am not responsible for the consequences, but the British Government. If anything had happened to me when I was last in prison, it would have been atrributed to John Maclean, not to those who are working in the interests of the Government. I have been able to lay down my principle and policy, not from mere internal and personal experience, but from objective experience. I studied the matter carefully, I combated the evils that were going to be perpetrated by the Government by reducing my food to the minimum, and the present Secretary for Scotland knows that when I was in Perth I wrote to him asking more food because of my reduced weight. I was about eight stones in weight at the time, and the doctor after weighing me, had to grant me more food. The food, however, was of no use to me. I threw it into the pot. My position is, therefore, that I take no more Government food, that I will not allow any food to be forced in upon me, and if any food is forced in upon me I am not responsible for it, but when the Government can launch millions of men into the field of battle, then perhaps the mere disposal of one man is a mere bagatelle and a trifle.

Russia's Fight for Freedom

So far as Russian freedom and British slavery are concerned, I wish to draw attention to the fact that an article appeared in the " Scotsman " the other day about Bolshevism, and I have a feeling that that article was written especially for this trial to create a feeling against Bolshevism. The statements in that article are a travesty. Inside Russia, since Lenin and Trotsky and the Bolsheviks came into power, there have been fewer deaths than for the same period under any Czar for 300 years. Capitalists have been killed perhaps, officers have been killed perhaps, because they have not submitted to those who have come to the top—the majority of the people—in the name of Bolshevism. Some may have been put to death.

When there was a shortage and disorganisation of the food supplies before the Bolsheviks came into power, there may have been individuals who, in their scramble for food for themselves, have gone to excess, but the crimes of individuals cannot be charged to Governments. No person would hold the Government responsible for the action of those individuals. The Bolshevik Government has not given orders to kill men. They have to imprison men until a complete reconstruction of Society has come about. It may be news to some of you that the Co-operative movement in Russia has grown more rapidly than in any other part of the world, and since the Bolsheviks have come into power, co-operation has been growing more and more rapidly. The universities have been used during the day, and in the evenings, to train the working classes in order that they may manage the affairs of their country in an intelligent manner. The schools have also been used in the evenings, the music halls have been used, and the theatres, and the picture houses, all have been used, not for the trivial trash which is given to the people of this country—but all for the purpose of organising the production of food and the work inside the workshops and factories.

We saw that prior to our comrades in Russia signing their treaty, when the Germans made their advance into Esthonia, Lithuania, and so on—the border countries between Germany and Russia—the Capitalist class in the respective towns had lists of men who were members of the Soviets, and those members of the Soviets were taken and put against a wall, and shot at the instigation of the propertied class of Russia. They have been responsible for more deaths than the Soviets. Our Finnish comrades, the Red Guards, have pointed out that the ordinary procedure of war has not been acceded to them, that as soon as the White Guards, the capitalist class, take any one of them prisoner, they immediately put them to death. It has been said that our comrades over there in Russia were working hand in hand with the Germans, and the proof of this was that the Germans allowed Lenin to pass through Austrian territory. Our comrades have stood up against Germany as best they could, and the capitalists—the so-called patriots of Russia—have been working hand in hand with Germany in order to crush the people of Russia. That has been done in the Ukraine. It has been done in the various States stolen by Germany from Russia.

FACE TO FACE

The Lord Advocate pointed out here that I probably was a more dangerous enemy that you had got to face than in the Germans. *The working class, when they rise for their own, are more dangerous to capitalists than even the German enemies at your gates.* That has been repeatedly indicated in the Press, and I have stated it as well. I am glad that you have made this statement at this, the most historic trial that has ever been held in Scotland, when the working class and the capitalist class meet face to face. The Bolsheviks got into power in October, and the people wished peace, and they were doing their best to get peace. The Bolsheviks wished peace throughout the world. They wished the war to cease in order that they might settle down to the real business of life, the economic reorganisations of the whole of Russia. They therefore got into negotiation with the Germans, and they and the Germans met at Brest Litovsk.

Towards the end of December there was a pause in the negotiations for ten days, in order to allow the British and their Allies to go to Brest Litovsk. An opportunity, therefore, was given to Great Britain to go to Brest Litovsk. Ten days were given. The last day was 4th January of this year. Great Britain paid no attention to this opportunity, but on 5th January Lloyd George, in one of his insidious speeches, seemed to climb down as it were. He was followed by Mr. Woodrow Wilson. But a speech by Mr. Lloyd George on the 5th was of no use. It was mere talk. It was mere camouflage, or, a better word still, bluff, pure bluff. Why did the Government not accept the opportunity and go to Brest Litovsk ? If conditions absolutely favourable to Germany were proposed, then Britain would have stopped the negotiations and plunged once more into the war, and I am confident of this, if Germany had not toed the line and come up square so far as peace negotiations were concerned, that the Russian workers would have taken the side of Britain, and I am confident of this, that the Socialists in all the Allied countries would have backed up their Governments in order to absolutely crush

Germany, and we would at the same time have appealed to the Socialists of Germany to overthrow their Government.

Great Britain did not do so. On the other hand, they came on with their Man Power Bill, and also with their factor of short food. All these things must be considered in their ensemble before you can understand the position taken up by myself. When this universal peace meeting was held at Brest Litovsk, then Trotsky played a very, very bold game. He knew the risks he ran. He and the Bolsheviks spread millions of leaflets amongst the workers of Germany in the trenches—the German soldiers—urging them to stop fighting and to overthrow the Kaiser, the junkers, and the capitalist classes of Germany. They made a bold bid by trying to get the German workers on to their side. Great Britain has been doing the very same thing since the commencement of the war. Great Britain has been trying to bring about, and hoping and urging for a revolution in Germany, in the hope that the working class would overthrow the autocratic class there and give us peace.

From a British point of view, revolution inside Germany is good ; revolution insider Britain is bad. So says this learned gentleman. He can square it if he can. I cannot square it. The conditions of Germany economically are the conditions of Britain, and there is only a very slight difference between the political structure of Germany and that of this country at the best. And so far as we workers are concerned, we are not concerned with the political super-structure ; we are concerned with the economic foundation of society, and that determines our point of view in politics and industrial action. Our Russian comrades, therefore, did the very same as the British have been doing ; they appealed to the German soldiers and workers to overthrow their Government.

Strikes broke forth in Italy. The strikes in January passed into Germany, more menacing strikes than have taken place inside the British Isles. An appeal was made from comrades to comrades. Many soldiers in Germany mutinied ; many sailors of Germany mutinied, and these men are being shot down by their Government. All hail to those working men of Germany who refused at the bidding of the capitalist to go on with this war. Their names will go down bright and shining where those of the capitalist of to-day and of the past will have been forgotten.

It would be a very bad thing for the workers of the world if a revolution were developed and carried through to success in Germany, and no similar effort were made in this country. The German workers' enemy is the same as our enemy in this country—the landlords and the capitalists are our mutual enemy—and if it was their business and their right and their duty to overthrow their autocratic government, then it will be a duty on us not to allow these men to overthrow their Government, and then to allow France, Britain and Italy to march over them and make these German workers slaves at the dictates of the capitalists of the other parts of the world. There was the situation from their point of view and from our point of view too.

THE CAPITALISTS ABOLISH THE CONSTITUTION

It has been pointed out that if we developed a revolution the Germans would come over and, instead of having liberty, we would be under the iron heel of the Kaiser. If I grant that that is true, it is equally true in the other case that the Allies would do in Germany what the German Kaiser with the capitalist class of Germany would do in this country. There can only be a revolution when the workers of all the countries stand united and capitalism is crushed, and until then the war must go on incessantly and incessantly. It is not because I am against my own people. My own people are the workers here, and the workers in Germany and elsewhere.

It was not the workers who instigated the war. The workers have no economic interest to serve as a consequence of the war, and because of that, it is my appeal to my class that makes me a patriot so far as my class is concerned, and when I stand true to my class, the working class, in which I was born, it is because my people were swept out of the Highlands, and it was only because of my own ability that I remained. I have remained true to my class, the working class, and whatever I do I think I am doing in the interests of my class and my country. I am no traitor to my country. I stand loyal to my country because I stand loyal to the class which creates the wealth throughout the whole of the world.

We are out for life and all that life can give us. I therefore took what action I did in the light of what was transpiring inside Russia, inside Austria and inside Germany. You have got to bear that in mind when you wish to understand my remarks. I therefore urged the workers of this country that if they were going to strike, mere striking was useless, because they would be starved back into work again, and that if they were going to be against the Man Power Bill, it meant that they were out for peace. And as there was no signs on either side of coming to an amicable constitutional conclusion, then it was the business of the workers to take the whole matter in hand themselves.

War was declared! no matter the motive, no matter the cause, all constitution and order was thrown aside, and in the prosecution of the war the British Government found it necessary to throw aside every law in this country and to bring in the Defence of the Realm Act, which means the negation of all law in the country. I have repeatedly pointed out that if the Government wishes to get a grip of any individual, they do so under the Defence of the Realm Act. The Government have power to do anything they desire. That may be right, or it may be wrong, but the position is this, that the bringing in of the Defence of the Realm Act has thrown aside all law and order as we know it during normal periods.

In the plunge into the war we have the abolition of constitutional methods, and therefore I contended, and I contend to-day, that if it is right and proper on the part of the Government to throw aside law and order—constitutional methods—and to adopt methods that mankind has never seen before, then it is equally right that the members of the working class, if the war is not going to cease in a reasonable time, should bring about a reasonable settlement, and a reasonable settlement to the workers in no victory to either side.

PROBLEMS AHEAD

If one side or the other wins, then the revenge will come, as France to-day is seeking revenge after the drubbing she got in 1871. Realising that, we, as representatives of the workers of the world, do not wish one side or the other to be the victors. We wish the *status quo* prior to the war to be re-established. If the workers are going to do that, then it means that they have to adopt methods and tactics entirely different from the methods which would be adopted, or could be adopted under normal circumstances. Abnormal lines of action must be taken, and I urge abnormal lines of action to be taken, such as our comrades in Russia took. The very circumstances of the war forced in upon the Russian workers' committees, and their national Soviets the line of the action which they adopted, and the only way we could do it would be to adopt methods peculiar to the working-class organisation in this country in the interests of the workers themselves.

The suggestions I made were intended only to develop revolutionary thought inside the minds of the workers. I pointed out at the meeting on the 20th that representatives of the police were present, and therefore if the workers were going to take action themselves, it would be absolutely foolish and stupid for them to adopt the suggestions I had given them. I only gave out these suggestions so that they might work out plans of their own if they thought fit to take action to bring about peace. I was convinced, and I am still convinced, that the working class, if they are going to take action, must not only go for peace but for revolution. I pointed out to the workers that, in order to solve all the problems of capitalism, they would have to get the land and the means of production.

I pointed out to them that if capitalism lasted after the war, with the growing size of the trusts, with the great aggregations that were taking place, with the improved machinery inside the works, with the improved methods of speeding up the workers, with the development of research and experiment, that we were going to have the workers turning out three, four and five times as much wealth as they had done in pre-war times, and a great problem would arise—a greater problem than ever before—before this country of disposing of its surplus goods on the markets of the world, not only of getting markets for these surplus goods, but of getting the raw materials. We see to-day in the committees appointed by the Government that they are anxious to get control of the markets of the world in order to exclude the Germans.

THE RUSH FOR EMPIRE

Our Government has already appointed a Land Organisation of the Board of Trade and of the Foreign Office whereby it is going to plant agents here and there throughout the world, so that in a scientific method British products may be thrown on to the markets of the world.

This is scientific methods applied to commerce internationally as well as nationally. These preparations are being made, it is being said, for the purpose of carrying on the war after the war. Nobody denies that there is going to be a war after the war, an economic war between the Germans and her friends, and the British and the Americans and their friends, and there is going to be a war between the nations, and the respective Governments will take care that, as far as they can, their capital will be planted in areas over which they have control.

You have, then, the rush for empire. We see that the Americans already have got one or two of the islands in the West Indies, and I understand that America has also got hold of Dutch Guiana. It has also been suggested that Mexico be brought into the American States. Britain herself is looking after her own interests. She has taken the German Colonies, she is also in Mesopotamia and in Palestine, going there for strategic reasons, but when Britain gets hold of Mesopotamia, Palestine, and Arabia, she will use them for her own ends, and I do not blame Britain for that. Britain has got many troubles.

We see Japan also on the outlook. Japan has been trying repeatedly to get control of Northern China. She would also like to get a great big chunk of Siberia. Even to-day we see the tentacles being sent out, all anxious to grab more and more power. We know the secret treaties and disclosures made by our Bolshevik comrades. We know that these nations have been building up their plans so that when the Germans have been crushed they will get this territory, or that territory. *They are all out for Empire*. That was absolutely necessary for the commercial prosperity of the nations.

All the property destroyed during the war will be replaced. In the next five years there is going to be a great world trade depression and the respective Governments, to stave off trouble, must turn more and more into the markets of the world to get rid of their produce, and in fifteen years' time from the close of this war—I have pointed this out at all my meetings—we are into the next war if Capitalism lasts ; we cannot escape it.

Britain had the wealth. Britain did everything she could to hold back the war. That necessarily had to be the attitude of Great Britain, but in spite of all Great Britain's skill or cunning, there has been war. I have heard it said that the Western civilisations are destroying themselves as the Eastern civilisations destroyed themselves. In fifteen years' time we may have the first great war bursting out in the Pacific —America v. Japan, or even Japan and China v. America. We have then the possibilities of another war, far greater and far more serious in its consequences than the present war. I have pointed that out to my audiences.

" NOTHING TO RETRACT "

In view of the fact that the great Powers are not prepared to stop the war until the one side or the other is broken down, it is our business as members of the working class to see that this war ceases to-day, not only to save the lives of the young men of the present, but also to stave off the next great war. That has been my attitude and justifies my conduct in recent times. I am out for an absolute reconstruction of Society, on a Co-operative basis, throughout all the world ; when we stop the need for armies and navies, we stop the need for wars.

I have taken up unconstitutional action at this time because of the abnormal circumstances and because precedent has been given by the British Government. I am a Socialist, and have been fighting and will fight for an absolute reconstruction of Society for the benefit of all. I am proud of my conduct. I have squared my conduct with my intellect, and if everyone had done so this war would not have taken place. I act square and clean for my principles. I have nothing to retract. I have nothing to be ashamed of. Your class position is against my class position. There are two classes of morality. There is the working-class morality and there is the capitalist-class moraltiy. There is this antagonism as there is the antagonism between Germany and Britain. A victory for Germany is a defeat for Britain ; a victory for Britain is a defeat for Germany. And it is exactly the same so far as our classes are concerned. What is moral for the one class is absolute- ly immoral for the other, and vice versa. No matter what your accusa- tions against me may be ; no matter what reservations you keep at the back of your head, my appeal is to the working class. I appeal exclusively to them because they and they only can bring about the time when the whole world will be in one brotherhood, on a sound economic foundation. That, and that alone, can be the means of bringing about a reorganisation of Society. That can only be obtained when the people of the world get the world, and retain the world.

The Judge pronounced sentence of five years penal servitude. Maclean then turned to his comrades in the court " Keep it going, boys ; keep it going ! "

INDEX